HOME FUTURES

the DESIGN MUSEUM

LIVING IN YESTERDAY'S TOMORROW

Edited by Eszter Steierhoffer and Justin McGuirk

Anna Sandberg Falk

Curator at the IKEA Museum

Sponsor's foreword

Last year, IKEA celebrated seventy-five years in business. For us, it meant a rare opportunity to sit down for a few moments and look back at our history. We spend most of our days looking into the future, trying to imagine the needs of people five, ten or twenty years from now.

What we have learned over the years is that people's needs are quite similar over space and time, regardless of where we live. Through our 'Life at Home' reports, where we interview thousands of people in their homes around the globe, we get an insight into people's needs, struggles and longings. We use this research to come up with new solutions to everyday puzzles. Our Democratic Design principles – which state that all products in our range must be affordable, socially and environmentally sustainable, have beautiful form, long-lasting quality and, finally, great functionality – guarantee that we stay on course in a rapidly changing world.

In the exhibition *Home Futures: Living in Yesterday's Tomorrow*, and this book that accompanies it, you will encounter many innovative projects and solutions that have been realised. But just as many wild experiments never went into production. We feel for them, and for the fearless creators who pushed the boundaries in order to invent something new and life-changing. We at IKEA have always been curious about innovative technology, inventing new techniques, materials and logistical solutions. Behind every single product lies years of research, experimentation and testing.

In today's changing world, characterised by urbanisation and technological invention, people's immediate needs change all the time. Does that also mean that the meaning of a 'home' is in flux, as this exhibition suggests? It may seem so. New family constellations are becoming more common, challenging the traditional nuclear family. Some people are constantly on the move, carrying not much more than a toothbrush and a laptop on their trips from town to town, while others leave the hustle and bustle of the big city for a life in harmony with nature.

It is our job to provide the solutions that make all of these life choices possible. For example, we are looking into rental or leasing solutions for urban nomads, open-source furniture that can be rearranged according to changing needs, small-space solutions for all of those with limited space in large cities, new tools for indoor gardening, and new technologies that make the everyday more convenient.

By partnering with the Design Museum, in the production of this exhibition and book, we are continuing our mission of cooperating with individuals and institutions that see the world from a slightly different perspective than we do. Through collaboration, we gain new insights into this crazy old world of ours. It is a vital part of our continuous learning process, and we hope it will inspire you as a visitor and reader as well.

Many western cities are now in the midst of a housing crisis. In Britain, the Thatcher revolution of the 1980s turned decisively against social housing and ended local-authority building programmes, making life endlessly insecure for those forced into renting from the market. Today, even the relatively affluent can no longer contemplate home ownership. In the face of all this, quite properly the debate has focused on how society can address the issue of scarcity. But it is not enough to talk about how much we should build – we must also ask what the home is and how we want to live.

Forty-six years have passed since the Museum of Modern Art (MoMa) in New York staged *Italy: The New Domestic Landscape*. It was perhaps the most ambitious attempt to explore new definitions of what the home might mean in the contemporary world. The Design Museum has staged *Home Futures* to bring the same spirit of enquiry to the idea of the home. The exhibition explores the domestic landscape through the lenses of technology, shrinking space, nomadic living and the idea of self-sufficiency – themes that reflect contemporary life but that also kept recurring in the twentieth century. It is through the radical visions of the recent past that we consider how our understanding of 'home' might be changing today.

The idea of home is at the intersection of community, privacy, comfort and status. It is shaped by emotions, memories and rituals. The nature of these qualities is both fixed and unstable. Home is the place in which we keep our photographs of our parents and, later, of our children; ancient school books and battered toys; and all the other things that we cannot contemplate parting with.

Home is intimately connected to our sense of self. To be 'at home' is to be yourself. There is no need for the mask that we wear in public when we are at home. In our quintessentially narcissistic world, no quality is more desirable. We now want to be at home everywhere we go, which is actually the slogan for one of Airbnb's advertising campaigns.

Despite its atavistic associations with the hearth and the rituals of domesticity, what we understand as the home as a place to live is essentially a modern concept. It emerged with the rise of individualism starting at the end of the eighteenth century. It is the product of a constant struggle between fundamentalists of various kinds who saw the idea of home as a chance to impose their sense of how life ought to be lived on others. For some, it was a political or moral issue; for others, it was a matter of business. Some were radical politicians, others were architects. And some were both. They offered competing ideas, from communal living to the ideal villa, from ostentatious display to restraint.

One of these fundamentalists was the artist Willi Baumeister. His poster for the 1927 Stuttgart Weissenhof siedlung is an expression of contempt for what he would have called conventional ideas of domesticity, but which was what most people would have seen as a model for home life at the time. 'How should we live?', it asks, and leaves us in no doubt about his answer. To judge by the blood-red cross that he has splashed across a photograph of a perfectly harmless looking Biedermeier interior, not in homes full of stuffy-looking wooden furniture. With his infatuation with the machine and the supposedly unsentimental attractions of efficiency and hygiene, he set a course that others would follow, from Buckminster Fuller to Reyner Banham.

Willi Baumeister, *Wie Wohnen?*
(How Should We Live?), 1927

The way that we live has changed as fundamentally in the last forty-five years as it did in the previous forty-five, between the opening of the Weissenhof siedlung and *Italy: The New Domestic Landscape*. It's a change that urgently asks us to question our understanding of home. Are privacy, security and memory fundamental human needs or are they reflections of particular moments in human history, to be discarded when they have lost their relevance? Is home still about our sense of who we are? We hear a lot nowadays about the 'smart home', but this is mostly led by the tech industry finding a new way to sell us products and consume our data. Then there are micro-apartments – an attempt to make urban homes more affordable (and profitable). But these are market-driven products, not ideas of home life. Apart from making homes smaller and smarter, what about new ways of living or new forms of domestic behaviour? This exhibition explores today's smart home, and finds that, for better or worse, it has radical precedents in the twentieth-century imagination.

Whirlpool Corporation,
RCA Whirlpool Miracle Kitchen
brochure, 1957

The 'home of the future' was a twentieth-century obsession. If the nineteenth century was preoccupied with history, the modernist belief in progress made the twentieth century particularly receptive to ideas of the future. As the myth of a heroic past was replaced with that of the future, these futuristic visions came to define the twentieth-century present. In the immediate aftermath of the October Revolution of 1917, the Russian avant-garde sought to break away from the feudal past and reimagined a new collective way of life that was no longer centred around the family unit. The resulting model of the Soviet *dom-kommuna* was a radical idea for a communal future. The post-Second World War 'home of the future' could not have looked more different. In the 1950s, a new consumer society was born and technological domestic consumer goods became synonymous with economic progress and the post-war reconstruction of the nation. In the 1960s and 1970s, the 'home of the future' became mobile. In response to the social and economic crisis of industrial societies, a wave of fantastical techno-utopias expressed a longing for a new place away from the home and its realities, and proposed a new nomadic lifestyle with no labour or possessions.

Today, the home is increasingly becoming an asset itself. In metropolitan centres, living space is shrinking with fast-growing urban density, and we are entering a new era in which most urban dwellers cannot afford to own property. As a result, collective and nomadic forms of urban living are becoming widespread. Our lifestyles become ever more connected on the global scale, and yet we are more socially isolated than ever before. Our homes are saturated with new technological devices and the boundaries between work and domestic life are no longer clearly defined. The home has been, yet again, reinvented as a centre of productivity. When looking at the contemporary 'smart' home, it is clear that the sci-fi of the 1960s and 1970s remains the main source of inspiration for the engineers and developers of Silicon Valley. *The Hitchhiker's Guide to the Galaxy* is Elon Musk's personal bible, while Echo – Amazon's smart speaker – was designed as the first attempt to create the '0.1 version' of the *Star Trek* spacecraft computer. Today's changes in the home are no longer driven by new visions of the future but rather by a nostalgia for our long-lost past futures. After all, our nostalgic collection of mid-century domestic furniture sits comfortably next to our high-tech gadgets in the smart home.

Home Futures: Living in Yesterday's Tomorrow compares today's realities with visions from the twentieth-century past, and, while referring back to those radical visions, it asks: do we live in yesterday's tomorrow? Are we fulfilling future predictions or,

1. Geoffrey Hoyle, *2010: Living in the Future*, illust. Alasdair Anderson (London: Heinemann, 1972), 4–7.

2. Such as Frigidaire's Kitchen of the Future at the General Motors Motorama in 1956 or Alison and Peter Smithson's House of the Future, presented in the same year at the *Daily Mail Ideal Home Exhibition* in London's Olympia.

rather, are we just stuck in the past? Ultimately, what does our nostalgia for past futures reveal about our present?

In 1972, science fiction writer Geoffrey Hoyle published a children's book with the title *2010: Living in the Future*. His account of life in the twenty-first century started with a brief factual description of the domestic interior of the future, which, according to Hoyle, was devoid of all basic types of furniture:

> In the year 2010 you do not sleep in a bed. There are no beds, no tables, no chairs. The floor is made for sitting, sleeping and walking on. It is soft where you sit or sleep, hard where you need a table or desk. Your home is carefully planned. No family lives in a house or apartment too large or too small for them. Every room has several uses. The bedroom is also an office, and the kitchen is a living room. In 2010, there are so many people in the world that every inch of ground must be used correctly.[1]

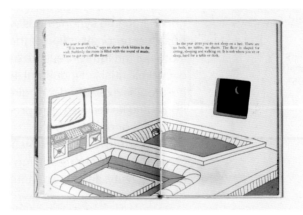

Geoffrey Hoyle, *2010: Living in the Future*, 1972

Hoyle's vision of the domestic future was inspired by rationalising ideas, utility and a wholehearted belief in technological progress. His detailed account also included a 'vision phone' that would have enabled e-learning, banking, shopping and work – all from the comfort of the home. In this hyper-optimised and efficient near future, goods would be delivered straight into one's fridge at the press of the button. All necessary domestic operations and appliances could be controlled from behind the 'vision desk' of one's home. This seamless image of the futuristic and ultra-rational push-button home was not only a familiar and commonplace image of popular TV shows of the 1960s, such as *Star Trek* or *The Jetsons*, but had also been an oft-rehearsed trope of popular exhibitions and trade events since the early 1950s.[2] Hoyle's book might be amusing for a twenty-first-century reader, but it would be even more startling for a time traveller from the 1970s to see today's smart homes and how many of the bizarre details of Hoyle's fantastical tale have been eventually realised.

The same year that Hoyle published his predictions for 2010, the Museum of Modern Art (MoMA) in New York opened its

3. *Supersurface* was commissioned by MoMA and produced in 1972 by Marchi Produzioni. It was the very first episode in the series later produced by Superstudio entitled the *Fundamental Acts*, which records the five primary acts of human life: *Life (Supersurface), Education, Ceremony, Love and Death*.

4. See MoMA press release no. 46, www.moma.org/momaorg/shared/pdfs/docs/press_archives/4824/releases/MOMA_1972_0053_46X.pdf [Accessed 8 September 2018]

seminal exhibition about domestic design entitled *Italy: The New Domestic Landscape*. Curated by the Argentinian architect Emilio Ambasz, whose afterword concludes this book, the exhibition set out to explore the global concerns of industrial societies through a survey of the previous decade in Italian design. The newly commissioned environments of the exhibition included *Supersurface*, a film and installation by Italian architecture firm Superstudio.[3] The installation consisted of a box of infinity mirrors with a geometric grid on the floor and clouds projected on the ceiling. It also included an animated film that outlined the designers' proposition for an alternative model for life on Earth, considering 'the possibilities of life without objects'.[4]

If Hoyle's book was exemplary of the modernist, utopian imagination and a celebration of the values and myths of the post-war consumer society, *Supersurface* – despite the seeming similarity between their future images – was its explicit critical counterpart. Superstudio could only imagine the future through a radical rupture with all historical, ideological and physical structures of Western society. The iconic drawings and collages by the Italian group are often compared with the dystopian images of Florence's 1966 flood, the worst natural disaster in the history of Superstudio's home town, in which the Arno River washed away possessions and temporarily erased most central areas of the city. Their concept of 'anti-design' would have meant the destruction of objects, and with it the elimination of all hierarchical power systems that man-made environments and objects have ever implied. Superstudio suggested a new kind of architecture for a new, egalitarian society that was to be freed from hierarchies, possessions and any form of labour. This radical political statement was first made explicit in their *Continuous Monument*, which would

Superstudio, *Life: Supersurface*, 1972

have replaced all man-made architecture with a global, non-hierarchical grid structure: a blank, featureless plane wrapped around the Earth as a continuous, globalising belt.

While never intended as a literal description of the future, *Supersurface* has become an apt metaphor for today's networked living. Its idea of the egalitarian grid has proved surprisingly reso-nant with the democratising potentials of the internet as well as today's ideals of a 'post-ownership' society, in which we no longer need to possess objects in order to use them. Today's internet-enabled sharing platforms allow whole new ways to collectively rationalise the use of available resources, which, in turn, enable an expanded definition of the domestic realm and increasingly nomadic contemporary lifestyles. But to what degree does an Airbnb-enabled lifestyle correspond to Superstudio's idea of nomadism? Is the post-ownership economy representative of the values once proposed by a life without objects and consumption? Has the internet enabled a more equal redistribution of power? And are we now more liberated (from labour, consumption and gender roles) as our homes are becoming smarter and more mobile?

The smart home has actually outsmarted its inhabitants, and the freedom of networked living has come at a huge cost in terms of personal privacy and data. *Supersurface*, just as much as Hoyle's sci-fi version of the smart home, is a familiar and yet a distorted representation of today's domestic realities. It is, however, these discrepancies between past fantasies and today's reality that provide a critical lens through which to reflect on the most pressing issues of our times. If Superstudio's project exposes the unexploited political potentials of today's transformation of the domestic sphere, Hoyle's futuristic rendering of today's domestic technolo-gies helps to reveal the ironies and inefficiencies behind our technological dreams. Looking back in order to look forward, *Home Futures* compares twentieth-century radical visions of the future with our contemporary ways of life. The comparison between the present and how it was once imagined reveals how our political and social ideals have changed.

Following social and economic upheaval, there is usually a retreat to the home. Traditionally, the 'home' is identified with a site of settlement and reconciliation, where wild things – and radical ideas – become domesticated. In the aftermath of the political upheavals of 1968, *Italy: The New Domestic Landscape* recognised domestic design as fundamentally reactionary, which, for a short while, became the main site of resistance and critique for so many radical Italian designers of the time. While this exhibition, an important reference for *Home Futures*, is mostly remembered for its experi-mental domestic environments by Ettore Sottsass, Joe Colombo or Superstudio, its main section consisted of the display of 180 household objects, which Ambasz organised into three categories according to their attitude to domestic design: 'conformist,

5. Emilio Ambasz, 'Introduction' in *Italy: The New Domestic Landscape: Achievements and Problems of Italian Design*, ed. Emilio Ambasz (New York: MoMA, 1972), 21

reformist, and contestatory'. As he optimistically remarked about his last category, 'The results of this mode of Italian design do in fact seem to correspond to the preoccupations of a changing society.'[5]

Alison and Peter Smithson, House of the Future, 1956

In a similar vein, the *Home Futures* exhibition and book explore the tension between the radical potential and the traditional idea of the home, and examines today's changing domesticity through contrasting prisms of utopian and dystopian visions. The exhibition is organised in six thematic sections. The first five present recurring – and often conflicting – themes of the twentieth century that significantly shaped our contemporary experience of the home: efficiency, minimal living, nomadism, self-sufficiency and the changing notion of privacy. The exhibition's final section questions the modernist notions of rationalising and optimising, and instead focuses on ideas of the home that, contrary to visions of progress, attempt to reinvent the domestic interior according to Arcadian ideals. *Home Futures* is not intended as a comprehensive historical overview of the domestic visions of the twentieth century, nor is it a chronological narrative of today's smart home. Rather, the historical case studies are selected based on their resonance with our contemporary experience of the home and its changing realities. The first part of this book, the Catalogue, is a visual record of the six sections of the exhibition, which comprise over a hundred historical case studies, prototypes, models, drawings and films, as well as pieces of contemporary art and design. The Catalogue is interspersed with entries from 'The Inventory' – each by a different author – that take stock of the changes that the contemporary domestic interior has endured in the last two decades. What happened to the TV, the telephone, the attic, the corridor, the bed or the screw?

The second part of the book, the Reader, includes six newly commissioned essays that set out to link historical case studies with our contemporary experience, and which further explore the

6. *Existenzminimum* is a German term that emerged in the 1920s to describe the minimum acceptable floorspace relative to the specific uses and functions of architectural spaces.

7. Hoyle, 46.

social and economic contexts of today's domestic realm. One of the central themes of *Home Futures* is the spatial transformation of the home. In the face of growing urban density, modernist optimisation of domestic living prescribed a highly functional approach to life and established a minimum for both the domestic space and its uses. The essay by Dogma (Pier Vittorio Aureli, Martino Tattara and Marson Korbi) explores the origins and the ideology of the modernist *Existenzminimum*[6] and presents a speculative proposal for the contemporary 'universal basic space'. A more fluid and hybrid architectural approach to domestic space is explored in Jing Liu's essay, which introduces the New York-based architectural studio SO–IL's residential projects, inspirations and understanding of the domestic ritual. SO–IL designed the *Home Futures* exhibition itself, and further explored spatial fluidity in the actual, physical experience of the exhibition. The translucent and immaterial quality of SO–IL's room dividers blurs the relation-ship between the inside and outside, and plays with our perception of architectural boundaries.

The twentieth-century dream of the home as machine finds its continuity in today's smart home. The technological transformation of our domestic landscape, and its social and economic implications, is explored from three different perspectives in the Reader. Adam Greenfield considers the underlying mechanisms that operate in the background of today's notion of domestic efficiency, and questions the productivity of our 'smart' labour-saving devices. Sarah Kember gives a feminist reading of the smart home. She questions whether labour-saving devices are still sexist, and whether the gender politics of home has changed at all since the mid-century renderings of the 'miracle kitchen'. The social implications of technological change are explored in Justin McGuirk's essay about domestic privacy, which argues that our traditional understanding of home as a private sanctuary has been replaced with a much more porous space, shared on social media and surveilled by smart home devices.

The final essay of the book, 'Irrational Home' by Barry Curtis, considers the twentieth-century home as a place where the past sits comfortably next to futuristic technological dreams and which, after all, still remains resistant to modernist rationalisation. What most of the techno-utopian imaginings of the twentieth century ignored was this inherently human nature of the home – a site of ritual and belonging, a sensory depository of memories. As Hoyle concluded his futuristic tale in 1972: 'However different the world in the year 2010, some things will stay just the same as they are today.'[7] No matter which year we live in, our basic human desires, needs and fears remain the same. Both the book and the exhibition conclude on the same question: whether the real, radical potential of the future of the home might emerge in the acknowledgement and embrace of the emotional and social aspects of human existence, rather than their denial.

CATALOGUE

LIVING WITH OTHERS

We think of the home as an inherently private place, where we retreat from the gaze of others. Yet the twentieth century produced numerous visions in which technology opened up the home to two-way communication – beaming the world in, and beaming the home out. In *1984*, George Orwell described a dystopian near future in which privacy had been made obsolete by ubiquitous surveillance. His sinister 'telescreen', which was both television and security camera, was a metaphor for surveillance by totalitarian regimes.

Various designers have explored the idea that the presence of mass media in our homes would transform our social interactions and private behaviour. Ugo La Pietra's Telematic House anticipated the proliferation of screens in today's homes. In his vision, all domestic activity was to be mediated through screens and cameras seamlessly integrated into the interior. Others imagined TV helmets and 'Environment Transformers' designed to stretch the boundaries of the home, promising an escape beyond its walls. These devices seem amusingly futuristic and yet reminiscent of our present-day use of mobile screens and other communication devices.

Today, the domestic interior is less of a closed world. We post pictures of our homes on social media and Airbnb. The proliferation of connected devices has made our homes into hubs of the emerging data economy. And the implications for the idea of the private realm may be profound. Smart speakers are always 'listening' in order to serve their function, and our homes are full of cameras and smart devices that hoover up data about our domestic activity. Has privacy turned into the new currency of the data economy? If privacy is fundamental to the idea of home, then do new technologies that monitor us undermine the idea of home as we know it?

LINEN CHEST HOUSE

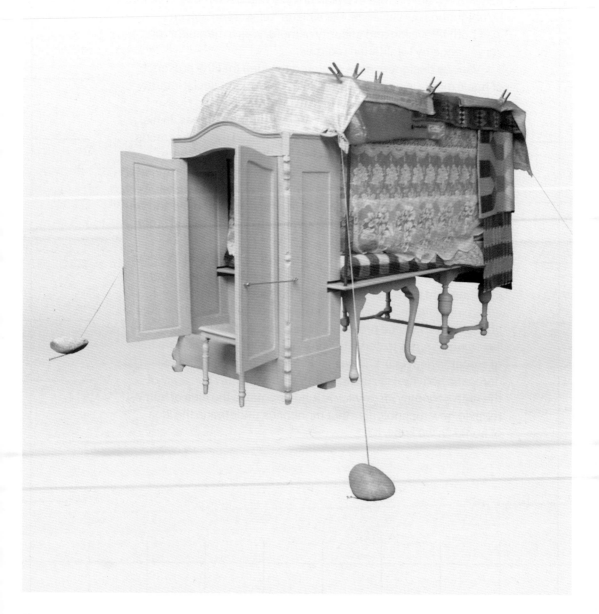

Studio Makkink & Bey, Linen Chest House installation, 2002

Our new dining server.

Johanna Pichlbauer imagines how we might physically
store our private information and data in our homes
rather than in data farms. At a time when most of
our private information, personal photographs and
correspondence are stored digitally in vast server
farms, Pichlbauer explores how design can respond
to the changing concept of privacy.

ELECTRO-DRAUGHT EXCLUDER

The Electro-Draught Excluder helps to deflect electro-magnetic fields that emanate from the electronic appliances populating our homes. In this speculative project, Dunne & Raby explore the anxieties and narratives that we construct around the presence of electronic objects in domestic environments.

Dunne & Raby, Electro-Draught Excluder
(Placebo project), 2001

EYE CLOCK

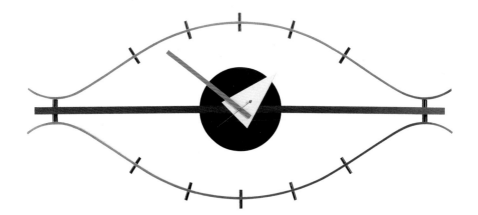

        George Nelson, Eye Clock, 1957

GLASS HOUSE

In sketches for his unrealised film *Glass House*, Sergei Eisenstein imagined life in a new type of building – a glass tower. Inspired by modernist glass architecture of the early twentieth century, as well as the emergence of the surveillance state in the Soviet Union, it was a formal and ideological exploration of transparency and privacy in the modern world.

Sergei Eisenstein, studies for *Glass House*, 1926–30

YOUR NEW CITIZEN ID IS JS0986D

Your upcoming citizenship assessment

HMCRO USE ONLY	
AG	ID
1	
2	
3	

Congratulations on your successful application to the Citizen Rotation Office, becoming a member is a significant life event. We have reclaimed the housing market and integrated the most established digital sharing services within our new Data Nationalisation government policy.

By enrolling you agree:

1. To the real-time sensing and recording of all your actions and the sharing of these records in public and private space.

2. To the healthy and safe distribution of your time and belongings (to be used by others as determined from your citizen profile).

3. To follow all directions and routes generated and assigned to you based on your needs.

HM Citizen Rotation Office

Luke Sturgeon, *Assessment Notice,*
Citizen Rotation Office, 2016

Warren K Leffler,
Crime on T.V. – children, 1964

... the television?

Television's arrival in the 1940s transformed our homes for the next three quarters of a century. Not only did it monopolise the way in which millions spent their leisure time, it also configured our living rooms in a highly prescribed manner: a centrally positioned TV 'set' with a sofa facing it. This was the only arrangement that allowed the family to bask in the warm glow of visual broadcast media.

It is no wonder, then, that this central messaging device aspired to the condition of furniture. How to introduce a machine into a refined domestic interior? By setting the screen in a walnut-veneer cabinet on legs. The artist Donald Judd wrote of trying to buy a TV in the 1970s: 'All were made of plastic imitating wood, some like your Anglo grand-mother's sideboard, some like your Italian grandmother's credenza, some like your Latino grandmother's aparador.' The idea that the machine had to disguise itself as a family heirloom was, says Judd, a product of 'the myth of the old home'.

In the twenty-first century, however, two things happened in relatively quick succession. First, television-as-object was replaced by the flat-screen. Now the question of design was redundant, super-seded by the fetish of resolution (HD, UHD, 4K UHD, etc). Every year, flat-screens got thinner and thinner, and bigger and bigger. Samsung's 9000 series, for instance, was 75 inches across – the equivalent of a shortish basketball player stretched diagonally across your wall – and only one third of an inch thick. Once the proud hearth of the home, the 'gogglebox' was now trying to replace the wallpaper.

The second, more important, thing that happened was that televisions started to disappear. The TV's aspiration to pure surface was consistent with the dematerialisation of objects in our lives more generally: the disappearance of diaries, cameras, calculators and so on behind the black glass of the mobile phone. But it was really the internet that killed the TV. We now consume media on a multitude of mobile devices: laptops, tablets, phablets and phones. Media has been decentralised in a watch-anything-anywhere culture. Television has lost its hearth-like status, and the living room furniture is ready to be rearranged again. —**Justin McGuirk**

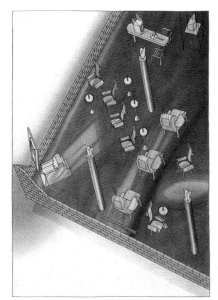

Ugo la Pietra, La Casa Telematica
(Telematic House) collage, 1983

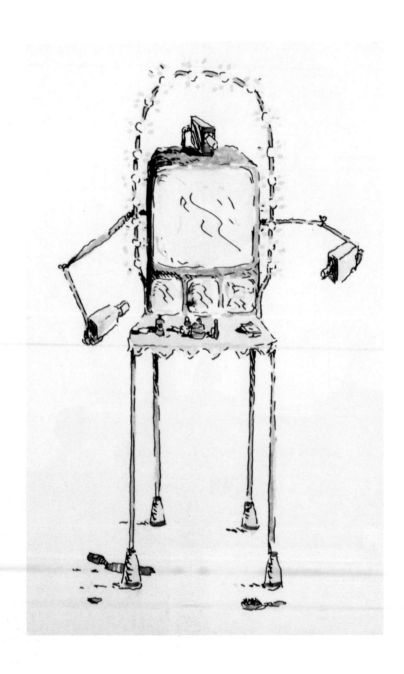

Ugo la Pietra, La Casa Telematica (Telematic House)
sketch (*above*) and drawing (*opposite*), 1983

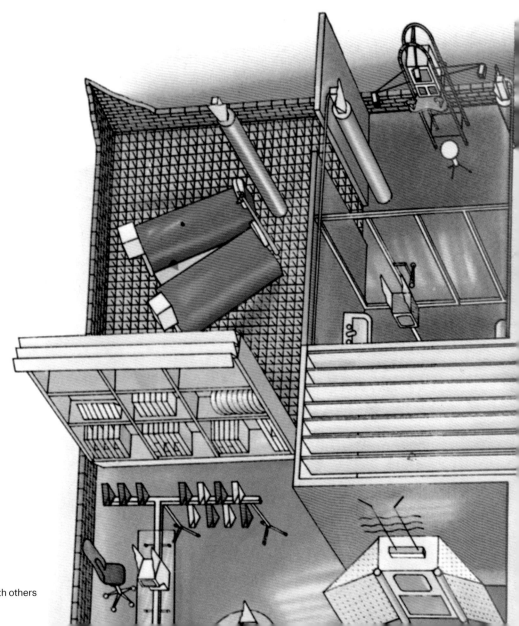

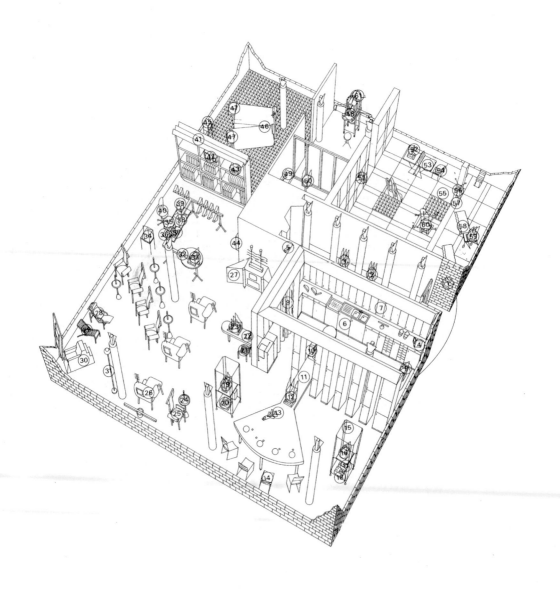

Ugo la Pietra, La Casa Telematica
(Telematic House) axonometric drawing, 1983

Ugo la Pietra, La Casa Telematica
(Telematic House), 1983

An installation at the Milan Furniture Fair in 1982, the Telematic House was an experimental exploration of the potential impact of communication technologies on domestic space. La Pietra's installation predicted the ubiquity of screens in our homes and questioned how they might change our behaviour.

Ugo la Pietra, La Casa Telematica (Telematic House), 1983

NEEDY ONE

Dunne & Raby's speculative proposal explores the potential role of robots in our future lives. Rather than performing tasks in the home and being efficient machines, these new cohabitants strive to respond to our emotional needs.

Dunne & Raby, Robot 4: Needy One
(Technological Dreams series), 2007

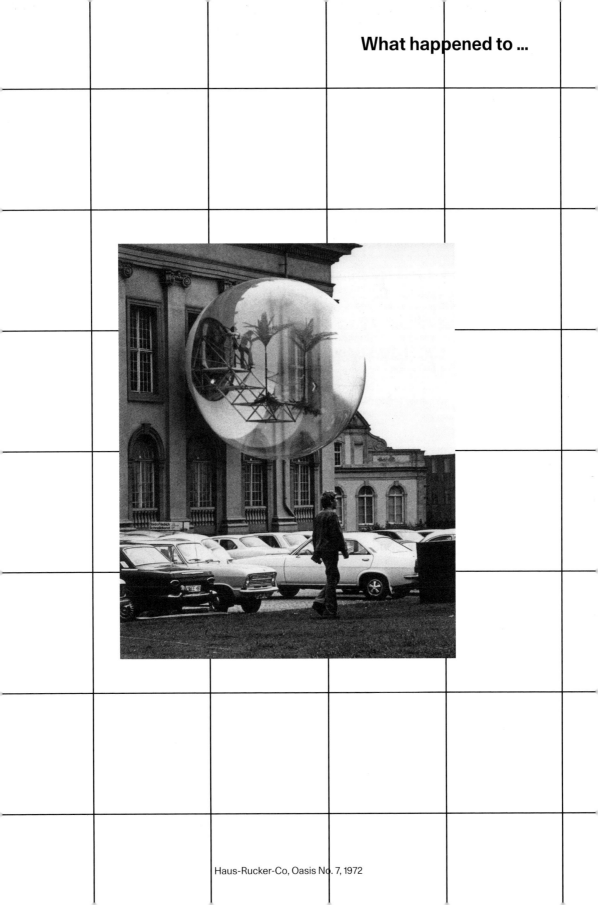

What happened to ...

Haus-Rucker-Co, Oasis No. 7, 1972

... the bubble?

'A home is not a house', claimed design critic and architectural historian Reyner Banham in 1965. Instead, he proposed we could dwell in an 'un-house' – a transparent bubble inflated by an air-conditioning outlet and centred around a technological core. This powerful image captured the imaginations of avant-garde architects and designers of the time. From 1967 to 1973 experiments with pneumatics proliferated, ranging in scale and form from Ant Farm's inflatable medical tent at a Rolling Stones concert, to Archigram's blow-up suit home, to Haus-Rucker-Co's bubble-shaped Mind Expanders. Coinciding with the worldwide 1968 protests and the rise of the counterculture, the bubble was soon co-opted as a potent symbol of rebellion. In the words of the Austrian trio Haus-Rucker-Co, in the bubble, society found itself in a 'softly flowing environment ... gliding into a different way of thinking on gentle wings'.

The idea of the bubble – transparent, lightweight, temporary and portable – has become an apt metaphor for creating space in a networked world, where communication technologies undermine the solidity of walls and borders. But with our societies more polarised than ever, it's not the solid walls that are proving the most sinister and divisive.

2017 was (unofficially) dubbed the year of the 'filter bubble', a term that describes the state of informational isolation in which we find ourselves due to the internet's algorhithmic predictions based on our likes, clicks and hovers. Following a series of elections heavily influenced by social media, the bubble swept international news outlets. Articles ranged from pessimistic, *1984*-esque predictions of a new era in propaganda and mind control to handy bullet points on how to burst out of one's web isolation. Today's social-media bubble ensures that we see the posts that we are more likely to like, hear political views that will not offend us and are offered commodities that we speak about with our friends. It offers comfort and convenience. In your bubble you feel at home. —**Anya Smirnova**

ENVIRONMENT TRANSFORMERS

These prototypes were satirical proposals for headsets that would alter our perception of the world. The Environment Transformers were examples of 'wearable architecture' that would provide new experiences by using integrated TV screens, microphones and speakers. These helmets are eerily reminiscent of our use of mobile screens and other connected devices.

Haus-Rucker-Co, Environment Transformers:
Fly Head, View Atomizer, Drizzler, 1968

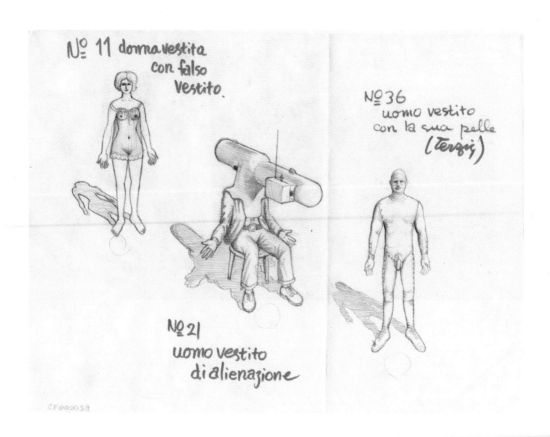

Tiger Tateishi with Ettore Sottsass, *Studio per Vestiti
e Svestiti (Study for Dressing and Undressing)*, 1979

Walter Pichler, TV-Helm
(Portable Living Room), 1968

LIVING ON THE MOVE

In the 1960s and 1970s, numerous designers sought to reinvent the home as a more nomadic and flexible space. Sensing that new technologies and building methods were around the corner, some, like Archigram and Hans Hollein, imagined inhabiting inflatable bubbles. Others conceived of modular environments that merged architecture with furniture, so that one could configure spaces in endlessly different arrangements for multiple uses. Ettore Sottsass' Micro-Environment, for example, imagined every domestic function as a series of separate but interconnected containers that could be moved around the home at will. Such fluid, nomadic conceptions of home were epitomised by Superstudio's collages of the *Supersurface*, which depicted a world without work or consumer objects, where all man-made environments would be replaced by a universal grid – a powerful network that would allow people to roam free and unencumbered.

Today, the internet and our myriad connected devices have made such notions of nomadic living quite plausible. We can live and work in a seamless flow from city to city or country to country. Now that our ability to feel at home is partially dictated by access to Wi-Fi and power outlets, the concept of home is arguably becoming less bound to a physical place. Meanwhile, the 'sharing economy' is gradually reducing the need to own so many objects. More people today own a mobile phone than own a home, and the familiarity of the 'home screen' offers a particular kind of homeliness.

So-called 'digital nomads' – normally young and tech-savvy – have embraced life on the move, but are we any closer to not needing the comforts of a stable home? And does the emerging concept of post-ownership make the traditional idea of a home less appealing?

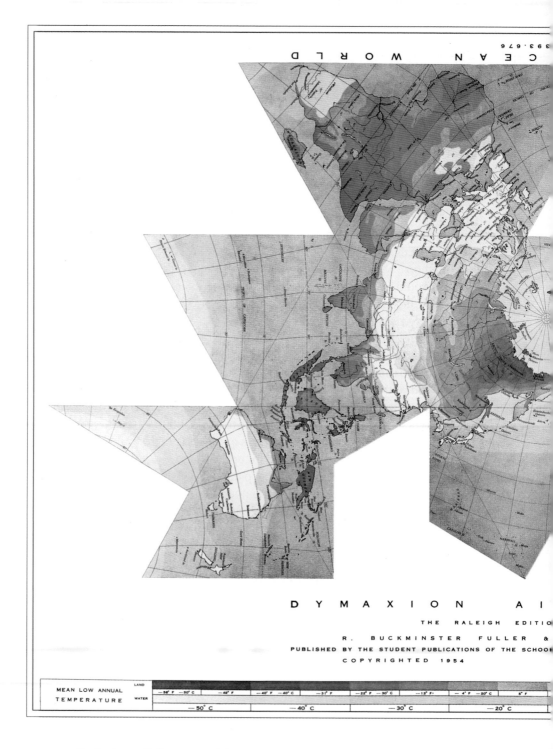

D Y M A X I O N   A I

THE   RALEIGH   EDITIO

R .   B U C K M I N S T E R   F U L L E R   &

PUBLISHED BY THE STUDENT PUBLICATIONS OF THE SCHOO

C O P Y R I G H T E D   1 9 5 4

| MEAN LOW ANNUAL | LAND | −58° F −50° C | −48° F | −40° F −40° C | −31° F | −22° F −30° C | −13° F | − 4° F −20° C | 5° F |
| TEMPERATURE | WATER | | −50° C | | −40° C | | −30° C | | −20° C | |

Buckminster Fuller mapped the entirety of the Earth's surface on an icosahedron shape, which, when flattened, rendered a map of the world with minimal distortion. At a time when the world was becoming more interconnected, it visualised the earth in a new way, providing the viewer with an unfragmented, global view.

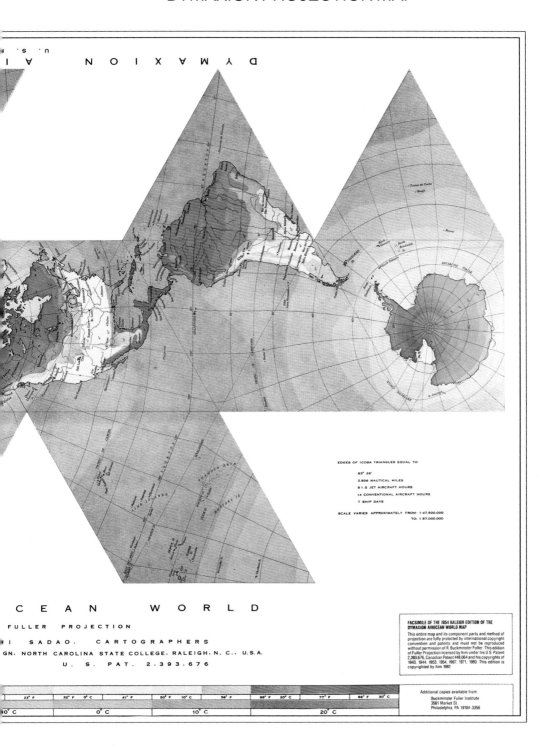

EDGES OF ICOSA TRIANGLES EQUAL TO:

63° 26'

3.806 NAUTICAL MILES

8 1:2 JET AIRCRAFT HOURS

14 CONVENTIONAL AIRCRAFT HOURS

7 SHIP DAYS

SCALE VARIES APPROXIMATELY FROM: 1:47,500,000
TO: 1:97,000,000

C E A N   W O R L D

F U L L E R   P R O J E C T I O N

I S A D A O .   C A R T O G R A P H E R S

GN. NORTH CAROLINA STATE COLLEGE. RALEIGH. N. C., U.S.A.

U.   S.   P A T.   2 . 3 9 3 . 6 7 6

Additional copies available from:
Buckminster Fuller Institute
3501 Market St.
Philadelphia, PA 19104-3356

| 23° F | 32° F | 0° C | 41° F | 50° F | 10° C | 59° F | 68° F | 20° C | 77° F | 86° F | 30° C |
| 10° C | | 0° C | | | 10° C | | | | 20° C | | |

Buckminster Fuller,
Dymaxion Projection Map, 1954

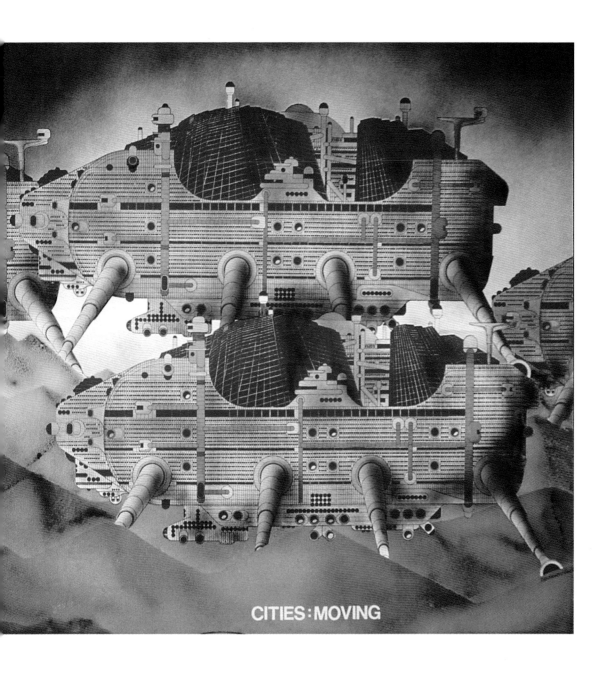

Ron Herron, Cities: Moving
from the *Walking City* series, 1963

IC IS HERE

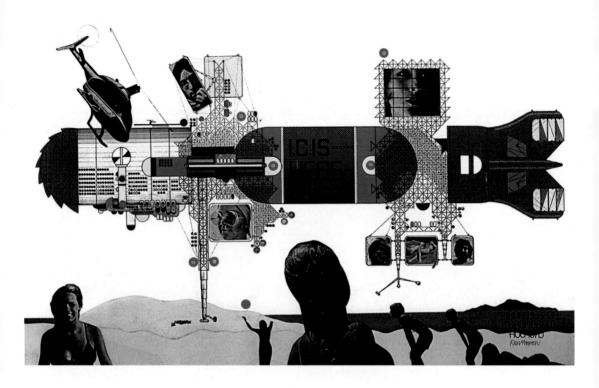

A speculative project by Archigram, Instant City imagined
an airship that contained all the cultural resources of
a metropolis. Moving from site to site and not restricted
by architecture, it redefined the city as an event rather
than a location fixed in space.

IMMERSION MAN EGG SPHERE

Ugo La Pietra, Immersione Uomouovosfera
(Immersion Man Egg Sphere), 1968.
A 'decompression environment' that offers
city dwellers an escape from reality

Hans Hollein, Mobile Office, 1969

MEMO

Ron Arad and Inflate, Memo, 1999

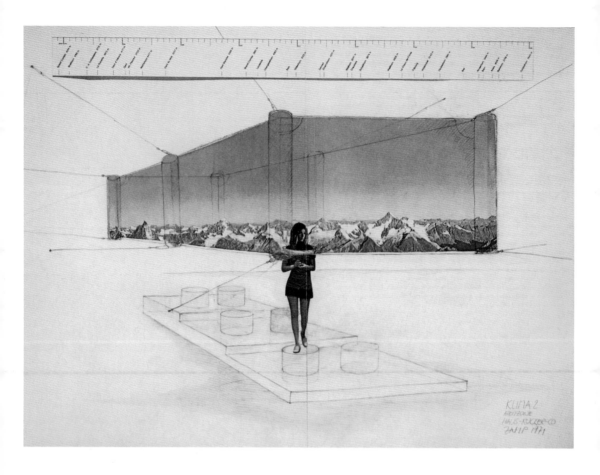

The Austrian design trio Haus-Rucker-Co imagined architecture without walls – a temperate environment achieved by using technologies such as air conditioning. Pneumatic structures, which proliferated in the late 1960s, were often seen as utopian proposals to do away with traditional architecture. *Klima* also responded to increasing anxiety about pollution and the state of the environment.

Haus-Rucker-Co and Laurids-Zamp-Pinter,
Cover: Klima 2 (Climate 2), 1971

What happened to ...

Cookes Storage Service, 2015

... the attic?

The attic includes memories; it is a place where your history is stored.
As apartments replace houses, attics are increasingly rare in city
homes. At the same time, there has been a proliferation of storage
centres, located not in the house but next to the highway; these are
industrial and simple. You can rent them where you like, close by or
far away. These places have become the 'new attics'. For the new
generation, the route to the attic isn't through their home but through
their towns and cities.

We might lament the loss of the 'traditional' attic. We might say that
these storage centres have no architectural value – they are cheap
and efficient but otherwise valueless. And yet, visiting this new type of
attic is still a ritual. Imagine all the amazing things that you might pass
on your drive through the city: so many more things than you would see
if you only travelled within your home. And then imagine the evocative
sound of the door to your personal storage unit opening, which is
actually very similar to the sound of a ladder being pulled down from
an attic hatch! And of course, in your storage unit you still encounter
your familiar possessions. These places hold not only your memories
but also elements of your future.

Even though the typology of the attic has changed, the ritual
continues to thrive. Soon the current generation might begin making
films and writing stories that depict storage units as the new attics,
emotive places where memories are hoarded and rediscovered.
Perhaps we should be thinking about how we design storage spaces in
order to acknowledge their role as part of the extended home. We can
learn from the home to create public spaces that acknowledge the
personal rituals that surround them. The 'extended house' can become
more of a reality. We no longer stay in one place; rather, our house has
a swimming pool at seven in the morning, storage at five in the evening
and dinner in the countryside at eight. Now we move constantly,
but we have a totally different and new typology of what it means to be
in the home. —**Studio Makkink & Bey**

MICRO-ENVIRONMENT

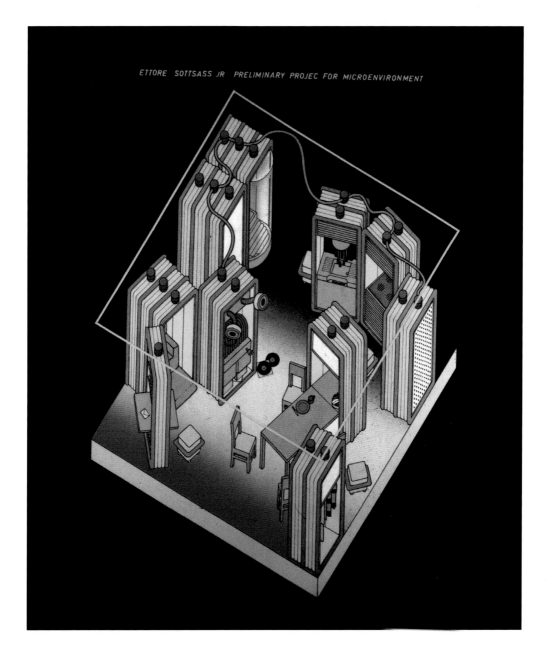

ETTORE SOTTSASS JR PRELIMINARY PROJEC FOR MICROENVIRONMENT

Sottsass's Micro-Environment, which was commissioned for the exhibition *Italy: The New Domestic Landscape* at MoMa, proposed a modular system that merged furniture with infrastructure in order to liberate the home from consumer goods. By using simple forms, muted colours and cheap materials, he framed furniture as a tool rather than a possession. These functional units could be easily moved around and reconfigured as new domestic demands and needs arose.

Ettore Sottsass, Micro-Environment
concept drawing, 1971

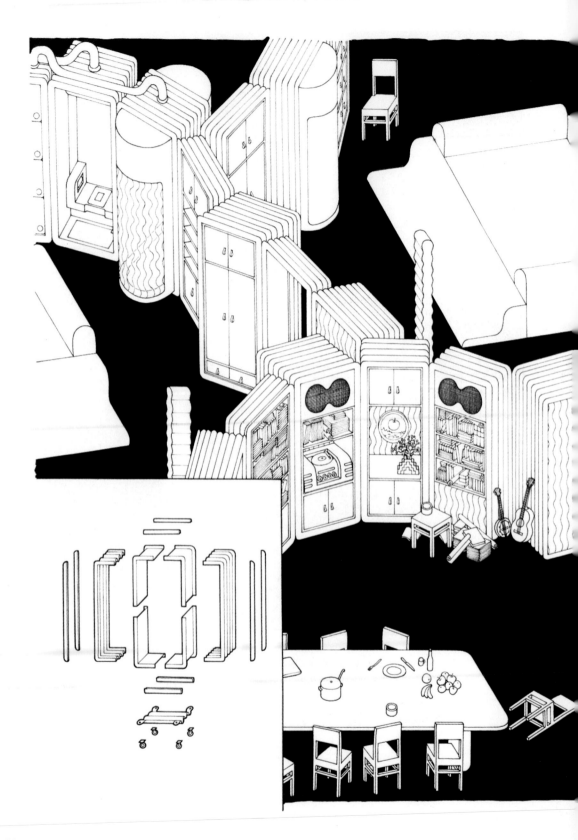

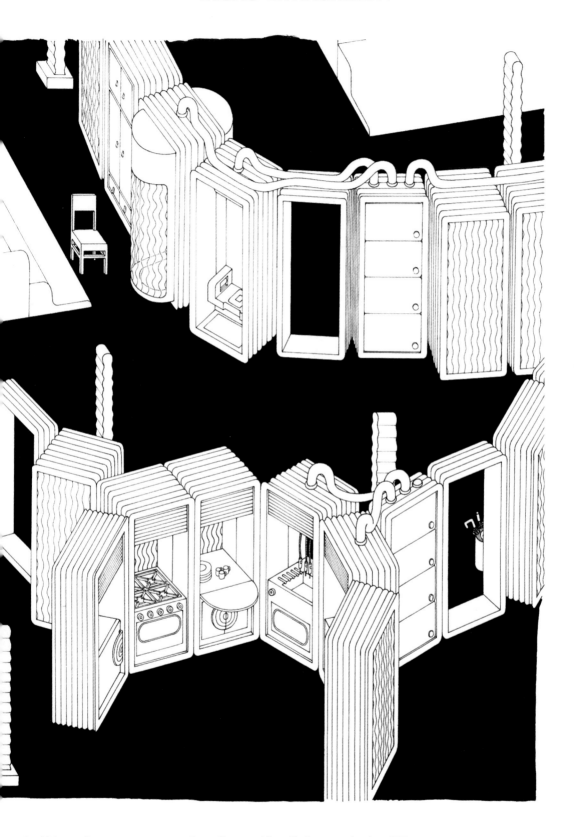

Ettore Sottsass, Micro-Environment drawing, 1972

single, triple and
double frame connected with clasps

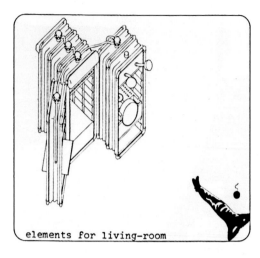

elements for living-room

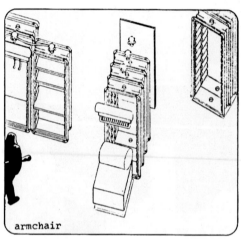

armchair

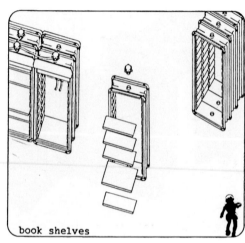

book shelves

juke-box

sink dishwasher

Ettore Sottsass, Micro-Environment drawings, 1972

Ettore Sottsass, Micro-Environment, 1972

Ettore Sottsass, Micro-Environment drawing, 1972

THE PLANET AS FESTIVAL

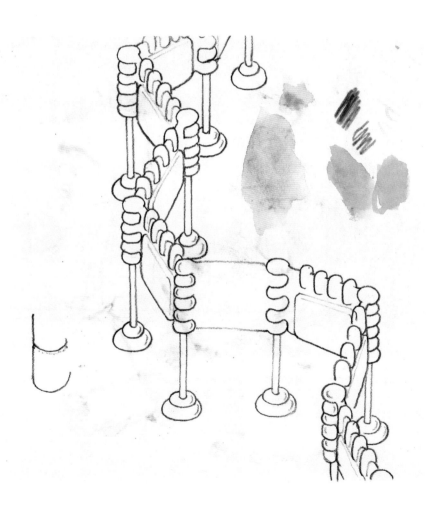

Tiger Tateishi with Ettore Sottsass, *Il pianeta
come festival: Studio per illustrazione
(The planet as festival: study for illustration)*, 1972

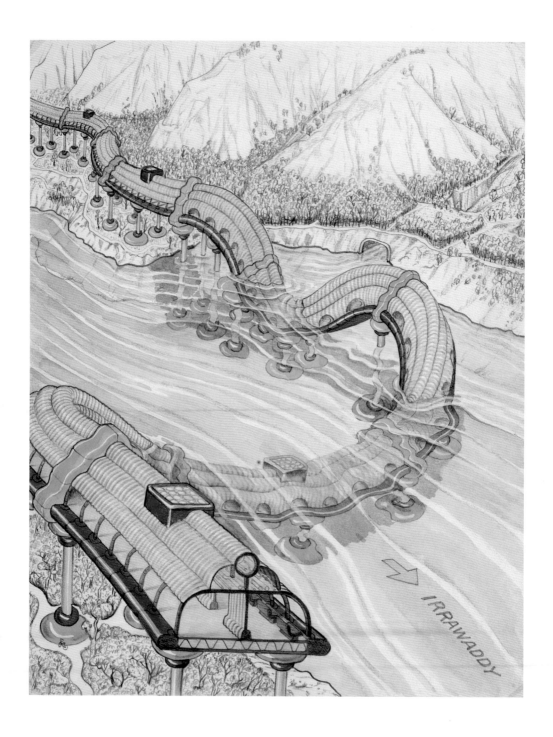

Tiger Tateishi with Ettore Sottsass, *Il pianeta come festival:*
Opera gigantesca. Strada panoramica per l'osservazione
del fiume Irrawaddy e della giungla lungo le sue rive
(The planet as festival: Giant Opera House. Scenic road for observing
the Irrawaddy river and the jungle along its banks), 1972

GRiD Systems Corporation, GRiD Compass,
the first laptop designed by Bill Moggridge, 1982

... the grid?

We can 'plug in' or we can live 'off-grid'. From the fields of urban planning to telecommunications to electrical distribution, the grid has come to symbolise connectivity and infrastructure, order and civilisation. In Superstudio's *Continuous Monument* of 1969, a homogenous, grid-like structure would sweep over cities and natural landscape. In 1972, the same architectural practice's *Supersurface*, an invisible and immaterial mesh, described as universal connective tissue or a network, was envisaged stretching across the landscape, promising a world without labour – or its fruit. Liberated from work and consumer objects, those two cornerstones of capitalism, the world evoked by the *Supersurface* offered freedom in the form of 'permanent nomadism' facilitated by this 'total system of communication'.

It is tempting to look to Superstudio's collages as prophetic. But what was arguably one of the first visualisations of the internet network as we now know it coincided with its development. ARPANET, the first prototype for the internet developed for the United States' military, was first presented to the public in 1972. Members of Superstudio, like most futurist utopians, identified their fantasies as 'admonitory tales' that spoke more of the present than of the future. They warned of the universal spread of industrialised, and increasingly hyperconnected, modernity – an ideology that the grid seems to encapsulate so well: electrical grid; urban grid; the grid of modernist architecture and painting; and, finally, the grid of fibre-optic cables connecting server farms and landing points where this infrastructure emerges from under the sea.

Supersurface imagined capitalist infrastructure drained of its poison – consumer objects. Today consumption has entered the immaterial realm, with images, words and symbols traded just as consumer goods were in the nineteenth and twentieth centuries. Today's network and an emergent sharing economy make possible Superstudio's 'permanent nomadism', redefining in turn our concept of home. For those privileged enough to be plugged into the grid, home can be anywhere – accessible at the tap of a finger or the click of a mouse. But 'to belong everywhere', to borrow Airbnb's catchphrase, means often to belong nowhere. When everywhere starts to look the same, whose home does it become? —**Anya Smirnova**

SUPERSURFACE, THE HAPPY ISLAND

Supersurface, first exhibited at *Italy: The New Domestic Landscape*
at the Museum of Modern Art (MoMA) in 1972, was a proposal for
a universal grid that would allow people to live without objects or the
need to work, in a state of permanent nomadism.

Superstudio, *Supersurface, The Happy Island*, 1971

"VITA (SUPERSUPERFICIE)"

Superstudio, *Life: Supersurface, 'Spring Cleaning'*, 1971

SUPER

SUPER

SUPER

Adolfo Natalini, drawings from
Sketchbook No. 7, 1968

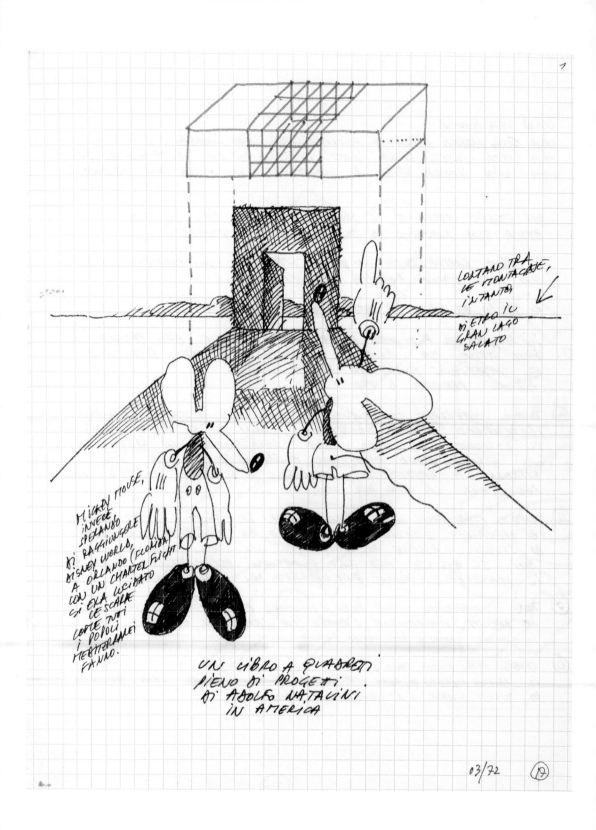

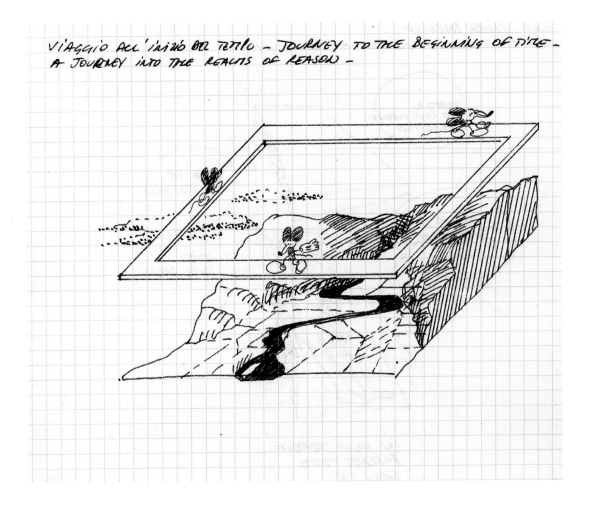

VIAGGIO ALL'INIZIO DEL TETTO – JOURNEY TO THE BEGINNING OF TIME –
A JOURNEY INTO THE REALMS OF REASON –

While Superstudio was overtly critical of consumer society, on his visit to New York to install the group's work at MoMA, Adolfo Natalini, one of the group's founders, incorporated images of American pop culture into his sardonic sketches of life on the *Supersurface*.

Adolfo Natalini, drawings from
Sketchbook No. 14, 1970–72

SUPERSTUDIO : LA SERIE MISURA   (1969-72).   Mobili e oggetti
Box alto cm. 60x60x174. Box basso, mobile bar 60x60x60. Scaffale b
Tavolo quadro piccolo 72x72x72. Panca, tavolo basso 36x150x36. Po
57x36x60, 45x36x54.   Ed anche fioriere, specchi, oggetti, multipli
MPL CENTRO INFORMAZIONI, VIA BORGOSPESSO 19, 20121 MILANO, TEL. 79

THE MEASUREMENT SERIES

ninato plastico serigrafato disegnato dal Superstudio per la PRINT.
0x60x60. Scrivania 180x81x72. Tavolo quadro grande 111x111x72.
ina 45x45x36+30. Letto 195x249x26. Tavoli sovrapponibili 69x36x66,

MERCOLEDI' 4 OTTOBRE, ORE 18.

Superstudio, La Serie Misura
(The Measurement Series) poster, 1969

Superstudio, La Serie Misura
(The Measurement Series), 1971

Studio Makkink & Bey, Nomadic Living, 2014.
A set of furniture imagining the contemporary nomad
in a pastoral idyll, with accessories produced
from natural materials such as wood and wool

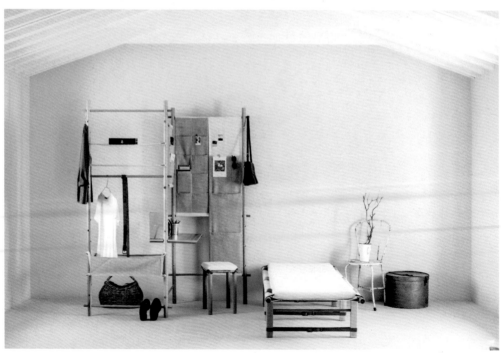

Elena Bompani, Itaca Nomadic Furniture, 2016

GPO, Telephone 746 in Olive Green, 1970

... the telephone?

Home ownership has become the preserve of the few, while phone ownership has become almost entirely universal. The phone became ubiquitous in British homes during the 1970s. Heavy, cumbersome and firmly tethered by a cable, the telephone sat stately and static in hallways and living rooms. These fixed phones anchored the home in place, making it a node in the wired network of telephonic communications, along which place-to-place calls were made between phone numbers registered to specific addresses.

The arrival of the mobile phone began a process of displacement. By rendering the landline obsolete, the mobile phone disconnected the home from the network that had anchored it, and made it easier for people to roam farther and more freely from the home. As the 'dumb' phone has given way to the seemingly endless functionality of the smartphone, the number of tasks that we need to be physically present in the home to complete have dwindled to a surprisingly small number. The processes of the home have reconvened on the home-screen. We can use our phones to turn the lights on, adjust the heating, put the kettle on, turn the oven off and answer the call of the doorbell – remote-controlling our home presence through the screen of a smartphone.

As the phone has become metonymical of the home, the home has gone mobile – transported around the world in our pockets. The phone is our home-away-from-home, for better and for worse. It powers the 'belong anywhere', utopian fantasy freedom of services such as Airbnb by offering a personal, (theoretically) private domain for us to carry with us wherever we go. A more dystopian vision, David G Morley's work with refugees shows how the mobile phone has come to embody the feeling of home for the dispossessed – 'a token of safety and belonging in a new modality of homelessness'. For the peripatetic – restless or precarious – the very mobility of the phone is what allows it to remain a fixed point, maybe the only fixed point, in an ever-moving existence: a screen so familiar that it feels like home. —**Mary Miller**

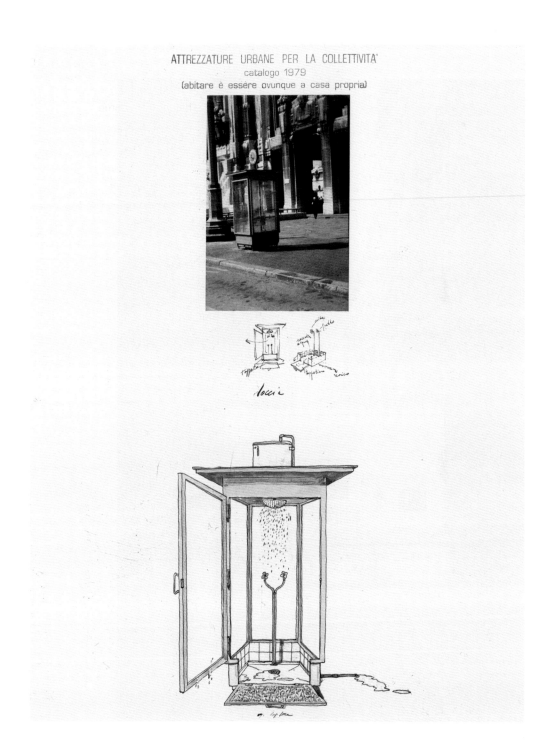

Ugo la Pietra, *Attrezzature Urbane per la Collettività
(Urban Equipment for the Collective)*, 1979

Ugo La Pietra, *Interno/Esterno (Inside/Outside)*, 1980

LIVING IS BEING AT HOME EVERYWHERE

La Pietra converted found objects from the streets of Milan into domestic items and temporarily inhabitable structures. His public performances turned the city's streets into a quasi-domestic setting, blurring the boundaries between the city and domestic space.

Ugo La Pietra, Abitare è Essere Ovunque a Casa Propria ('Living is Being at Home Everywhere'), 1979

LIVING SMART

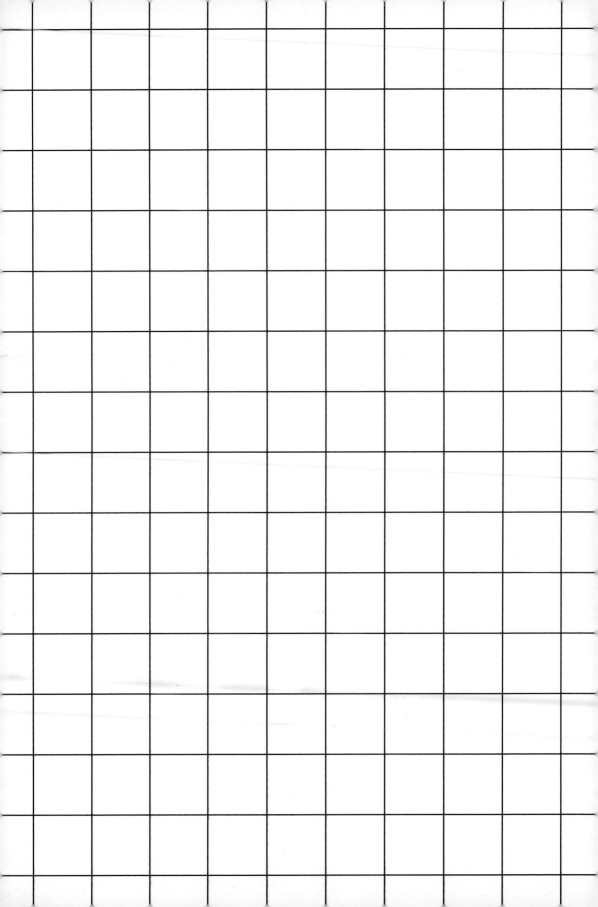

Push-button fantasies were common to the 1950s 'home of the future'. The modernist vision of efficiency and progress produced streamlined consumer goods and labour-saving devices that promised to make the housewife's life easier. The RCA Whirlpool Miracle Kitchen, for instance, envisioned a home fully controlled through a central computer. With such miracle devices as the radio-controlled vacuum cleaner, the ancestor of today's Roomba robot, domestic work could be outsourced to the machines. Villa Arpel in Jacques Tati's film *Mon Oncle* takes the idea of mechanical optimisation to its logical extreme. Ridiculing the modernist efficiency drive, this fictional house suggests that labour-saving might be more work than we think.

In the twenty-first century, the fully automated home has evolved into the 'smart home'. Here, the principles of efficiency and time-saving remain central to the offer but, with the 'internet of things', they are achieved by connected devices that use our data to predict our habits and preferences. This vision may have abandoned the futuristic aesthetics of the 1950s, but the gendering of domestic roles is still the heart of the home – most smart speakers opt for a female voice.

However, do 'smart' devices transform the home from a place of chores into one of ease and leisure? Some studies suggest that domestic labour still takes just as much time as it did fifty years ago.

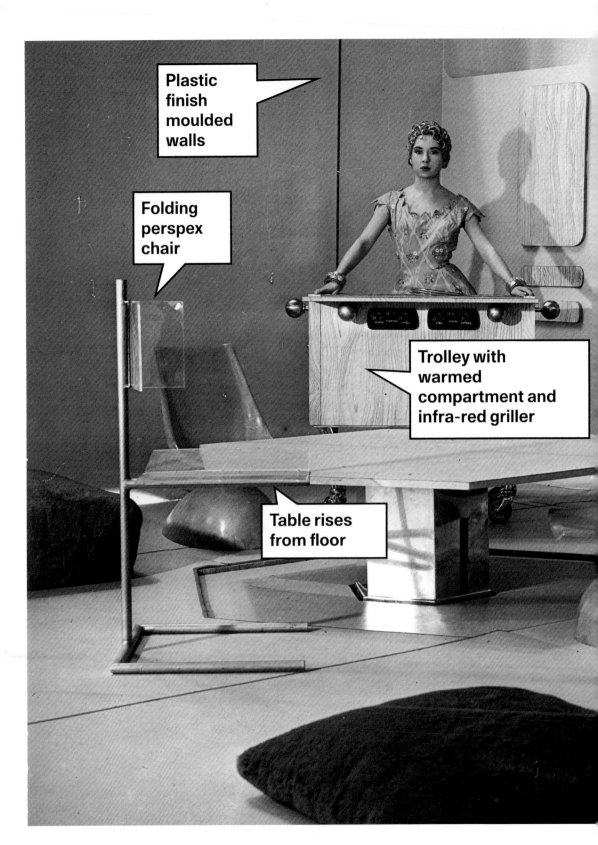

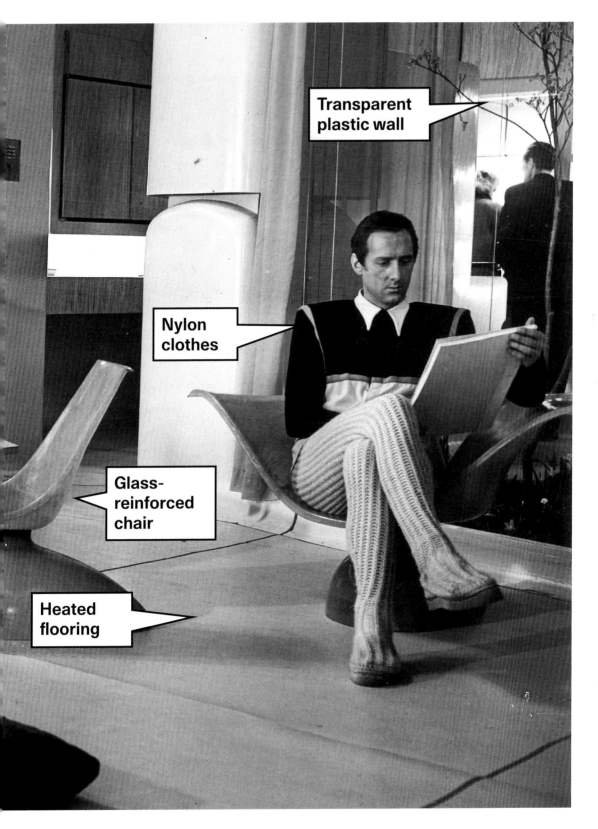

Transparent plastic wall

Nylon clothes

Glass-reinforced chair

Heated flooring

Alison and Peter Smithson, House of the Future, 1956

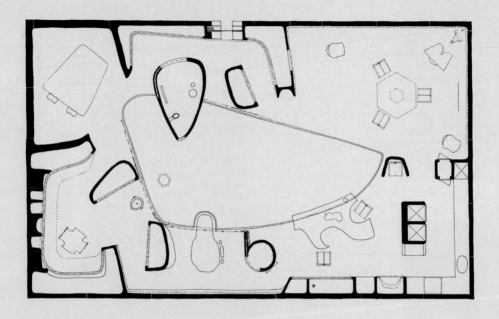

½"   DIAGRAMMATIC MIDDLE PLAN LEVEL HF9201

Alison and Peter Smithson's House of the Future imagined
a house fully equipped with mechanised furniture,
after-shower air body dryers, and an intercom system that
transmitted calls throughout the premises. A full-scale
model of the house was exhibited in 1956 at the *Daily Mail
Ideal Home Exhibition* at London's Kensington Olympia
and inhabited by a 'childless couple from the future' dressed
in futuristic costumes.

Alison and Peter Smithson, House of the Future plan, 1956

Alison and Peter Smithson, House of the Future, 1956

Whirlpool Corporation,
RCA Whirlpool Miracle Kitchen, 1959

PERAMBULATING KITCHEN APPLIANCES

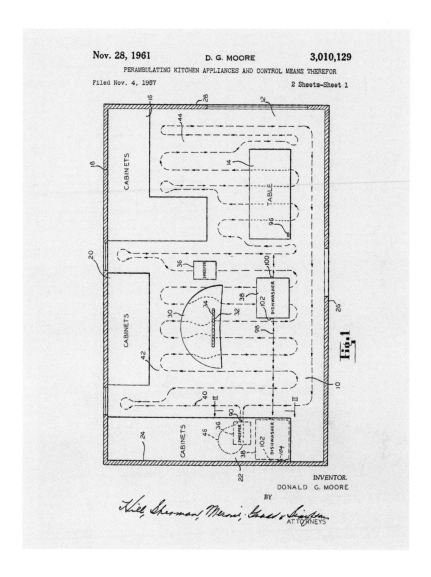

Exhibited at the *American National Exhibition* held in Moscow in 1959, the RCA Whirlpool Miracle Kitchen showcased a post-war North American version of the future. Features included an autonomous, radio-controlled vacuum cleaner; adjustable sinks; and a dishwasher that moved around the kitchen on an electric track.

Donald G Moor, Perambulating Kitchen Appliances patent, 1961

iRobot, Roomba i7+, 2018.
Autonomous robotic vacuum cleaner

Hanna-Barbera, *The Jetsons*, 1962–63

Modularity is Interaction is a playful exploration of
the relationship between human and machine.
The installation consists of a series of interconnected
modules and pendulums, each in a different shape
and size. Once activated, a chain reaction is triggered
and the modules swing into motion, one after the
other, as in a mechanical ballet.

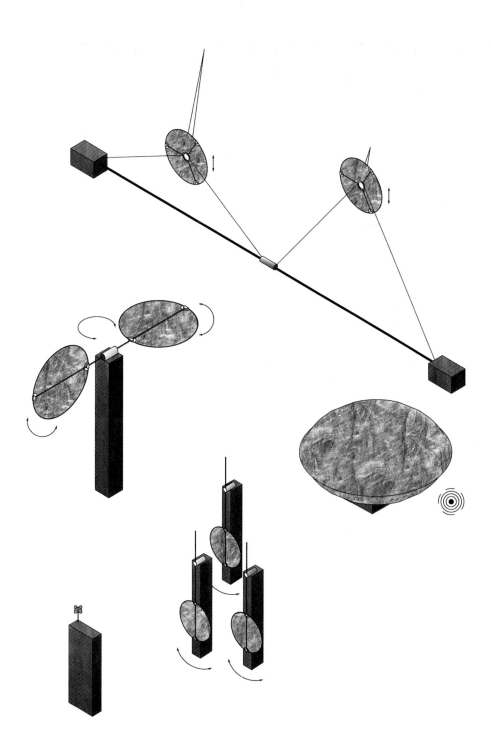

Dimitri Bähler, *Modularity is Interaction*, 2015

W Heath Robinson, *How to Dispense
with Servants in the Bedroom*, 1933

Light switch, 2014

... the light switch?

The inventor of the light switch, John Henry Holmes, was a Quaker, and thus a believer in the ability of each person to access 'the light within'. The light switch, of course, enables each person to access the light without, and has been doing so, solidly, since 1884.

That is, until the emergence of the voice- or presence-activated smart-home version – a brave solution to an unspecified problem. Holmes's switch is a simple design that has lasted for over a century. Entering an old house, we brush our fingertips over the wall in the gloom, caressing plaster or brick or wood before brushing against an early plastic, or even Bakelite, panel. The switch itself still tends to be firm, the ever-so-slight sensation of rolling as it moves to form a circuit – one of the most pleasingly robust 'actions' that an industrial designer could imagine.

Finnish architect Juhani Pallasmaa has declared that the door handle is the 'handshake of the building'; is the light switch the equivalent for the room? Pallasmaa noted that touch is a key part of remembering and understanding, that 'tactile sense connects us with time and tradition'. When you touch a light switch, you are sensing the presence of others. You are also touching infrastructure, the network of cables twisting out from our houses, from the writhing wires under our fingertips to the thicker cables, like limbs, out into the countryside, into the National Grid.

If we always replace touch with voice activation, or simply with our presence, we are barely thinking or understanding, placing things out of mind. We lose another element of our physicality. No sense of patina develops except in invisible lines of code, datapoints feeding imperceptible learning systems. As is often the case with smart systems, it is an individualising interface, revealing no trace of others.

And how dull rooms will become if they are always automatically bright upon entering. The cornerstone of most horror movies would vanish overnight.

We can only praise shadows if we understand them. The everyday light switch connects us to our daily infrastructure and the lives of others, with humble analogue intensity. —**Dan Hill**

HOUSE FOR A HELICOPTER PILOT

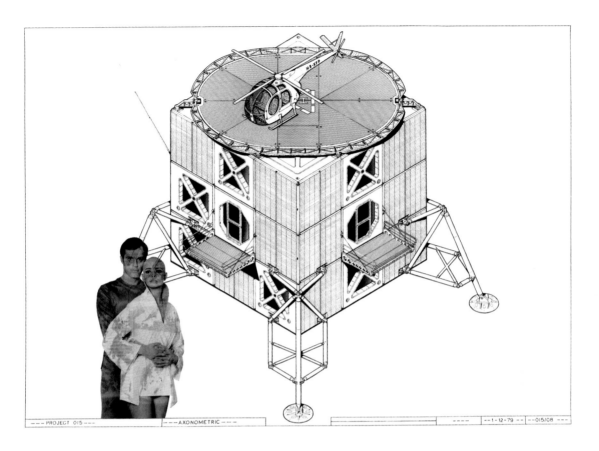

PROJECT 015 — — — AXONOMETRIC — — — — — 1-12-79 — — 015/08 —

Kaplický's *House for a Helicopter Pilot* includes a rooftop landing deck, lunar-module feet and integrated solar panels. Adopting construction methods from the fields of aircraft and car design, Future Systems (Kaplický's architecture studio) fused this high-tech aesthetic with residential architecture. Kaplický's collages turn the home into a machine to live in.

Jan Kaplický, *House for a Helicopter Pilot*, 1979

Jan Kaplický, *House for a Helicopter Pilot*, 1979

Heath Robinson's playful drawings illustrate absurdly complex contraptions, conceived to perform simple tasks. In these complicated devices, one step leads to another in a domino-like effect, achieving a small task (like lifting a razor blade off the floor) in an over-complicated manner. Taking the idea of domestic comfort to its extreme, these drawings mock the mechanisms of labour-saving.

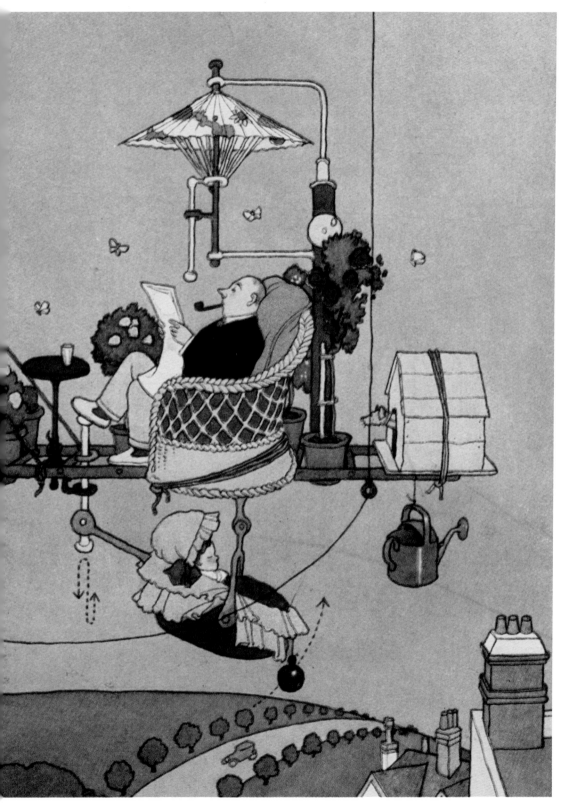

W Heath Robinson, *An Ideal Home no. II.*
The Folding Garden, 1933

NOSTALGI
sofa
Essential Life Stream interoperable sofa for the well-being of you and your family for now and forever. No shared ownership of activity streams with single domicile subscriptions. Configurable color and pattern schemes by Olafur Elliason™ change in real-time to suit your temperament with Philips Medical Inductive Mood Sense-Storage (Subscription fees apply.) Compatible with most modern charging systems. White. 000.000.01

52399:−

A design fiction IKEA catalogue
for the smart home of the near future

WELLBEING **2**

-15°C

12%

The more you capture your experiences, the more wealth you create from your data analytics. When and where you sit, what and how you cook for dinner, your sleep patterns and movements in bed, the patterns of foot-falls on area rugs and carpets, when and how you open doors, how and of what sort of bathroom behaviors — all of these can be captured, analyzed, shared and sold. IKEA is the #1 source of beautifully designed, well-constructed and assembled essentials for your home that give you control over your sensed behaviors.

Ari Birnbaum,
The Data Wealth King. Author,
Speaker, Commentator.

Mobile Life Research Centre,
Boris Design and Near Future Laboratory,
IKEA Catalogue for the Near Future, 2015

3 WELLBEING

LIV
MoSS® carpet
Semi-organic "moss"-like carpet that grows slowly over your existing flooring while also producing environmental cleansing and scrubbing characteristics. LIV is the natural way to enhance the air in your home by creating a biosynthetic effervescent plume of aromatherapeutic compounds making your habitat sustainable, healthful, comfortable underfoot and absorbent.

6.99:-/sq meter

NEW ITEM
The LIV shampoo and conditioner grow themselves saving ordering and hassles of running short. Re-grows and replenishes naturally, organically through safe, secure biosynthesis and genetic regeneration.

LIV
Shampoo & Conditioner
Eco friendly, self-replenishing from bio-generating base starter compounds. Never run out, ever. Lifetime subscription only.
LIV Shampoo. 800.456.20
LIV Conditioner. 800.456.21

9.99:-*/month

* Lifetime only.

Mobile Life Research Centre,
Boris Design and Near Future Laboratory,
IKEA Catalogue for the Near Future, 2015

... the apron?

The man apron is now officially a 'thing'. Fashioned out of hardwearing fabric such as canvas or jean, the man apron is as much a badge of hipster culture and the creative classes as coffee or a beard. Shoreditch-based shop Labour and Wait offers one of the best-known models, a bib apron made of Cotton Duck fabric, brass eyelets and herringbone-tape ties. On the company's website, a male model wears the apron outdoors and holds a pair of shears, as if to confirm the virility of his work. Yet Labour and Wait makes clear that its aprons are intended not only for workshop and garden but for the domestic kitchen as well.

While the rise of the man apron seems to announce the entry of a new generation of men into the kitchen, the question remains: on what terms? Do they come as conquering chef-heroes, armed with a battery of Japanese knives and stainless-steel appliances? Or do they come prepared to shoulder a more equal share of the housework, which is still disproportionately carried by women?

Rather than treating the man apron as an accurate index of real shifts in housework, it might be more productive to think of it in representational terms. When men are shown at home in aprons, it is typically to dramatise a profound threat or crisis in male identity.

Even though over the decades men have begun to shoulder more of the home burden, the supposed lack of male domestic skills has remained the subject of a stream of satirical Hollywood films, notably *Mr. Mom* (1983), in which a bewildered Michael Keaton – clad in a droopy, dirty apron – struggles to look after his children when his wife returns to corporate life. *Mr. Mom* riffs off the notion that somehow men are not biologically suited to nurture, cook or clean, at once exposing the stereotype while restating it.

When set against such bumbling portrayals, the man apron phenomenon begins to seem much more purposeful and positive. Even if the reality might take some time to catch up, there is something radical about the man apron's assertion of male domestic competence – so at odds with *Mr. Mom* – a signal that the new generation of men are prepared to roll up their sleeves and get to work in the home, the threat to their masculinity now warded off by tough, canvas folds. —**Barbara Penner**

MPO Productions and General Motors,
Design for Dreaming promotional image, 1956.
A film produced for the annual Motorama trade fair,
promising a future in which the automatic kitchen would turn
cooking and cleaning into playful and fun activities

JUST WHAT IS IT THAT MAKES TODAY'S HOMES SO DIFFERENT, SO APPEALING?

Richard Hamilton, *Just what is it that makes today's homes so different, so appealing?*, 1956

JUST WHAT IS IT THAT MAKES TODAY'S HOMES SO DIFFERENT?

One of the iconic images of British post-war art, Hamilton's collage *Just what is it that makes today's homes so different, so appealing?* was first exhibited at *This is Tomorrow* at the Whitechapel Gallery. Inspired by advertisement images of the time, the collage shows a domestic interior filled with consumer goods and images of popular culture and modern technology. These images were found in American magazines which, for Hamilton, defined the new iconography of the modern world. In Hamilton's 1992 remake of his 1956 collage, entitled *Just what is it that makes today's homes so different?*, the categories of items depicted remain the same, while the appliances and figures are replaced with new images, testifying to the endurance of consumer society.

Richard Hamilton, *Just what is it that makes today's homes so different?*, 1992

UNTITLED

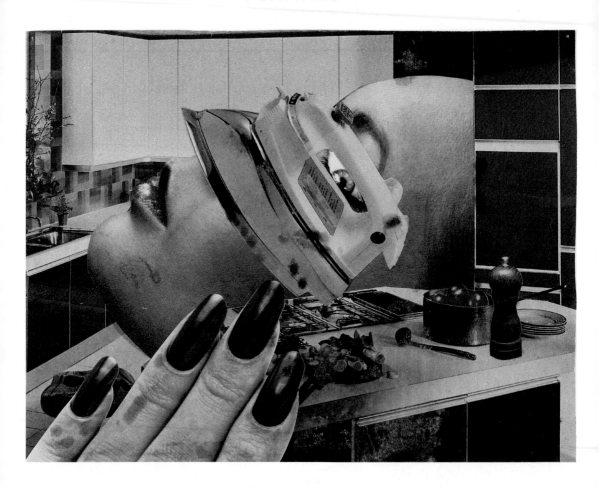

British artist Linder fuses sexualised images of the female body with homeware appliances like irons, toasters and mixers. Commenting on the gendering of labour-saving devices that became associated with women's roles in the home, her work offers a feminist critique of domestic labour and technology.

Linder, *Untitled* (Poor Thing series), 1977

IT'S THE BUZZ, COCK!

Linder, *It's The Buzz, Cock!*, 1977

BOCCA SOFA

Studio 65, Bocca sofa, 1970

Archigram's *The Electronic Tomato* is a satire on the futuristic, labour-saving devices of the 1950s. This fantastical tomato-shaped domestic robot would be equipped with built-in optical range-finder, TV camera and magic-eye bump detectors.

Warren Chalk and David Greene of Archigram,
The Electronic Tomato, 1969

Tools for Life is a mechanised furniture system designed by
OMA. The counter can move around and turn into a series
of benches, shelves or desks. OMA's furniture is conceived
as an instrument rather than a design statement.

OMA, Counter (Tools for Life series), 2013

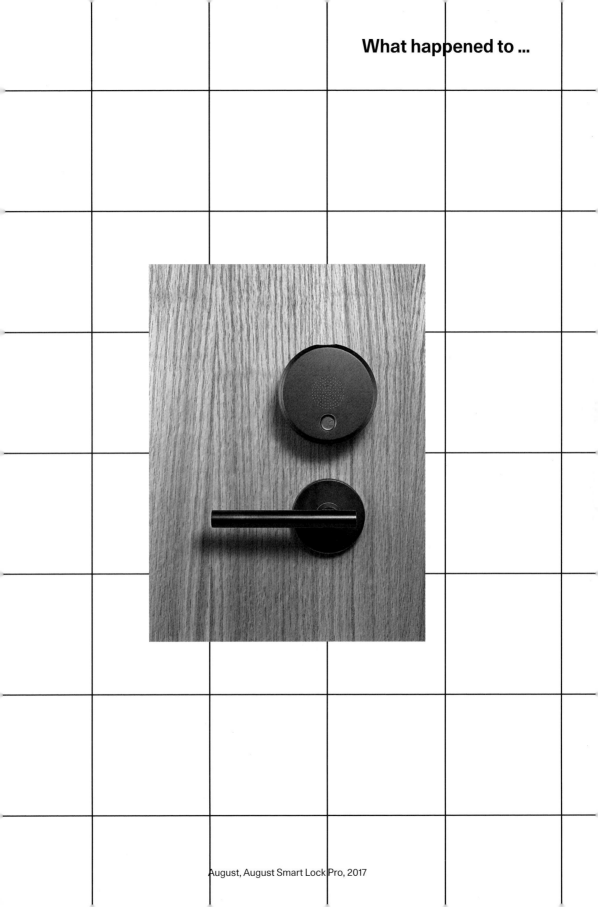

August, August Smart Lock Pro, 2017

... the doorknob?

'Your lock acts as your personal doorman. View real time videos of your guests on your phone. Your lock recognises you as you approach and lets you in, like your own doorman. You never need worry about whether you've locked the door, operate the doorman from your phone wherever you are. The doorman. The end of all your security worries.'

The heating was turned up to 'toast'. The bastard had whacked it up remotely again. She went to open the windows but he'd locked them shut on his phone. The film of clammy sweat was densifying into droplets, soaking through her T-shirt. She went to get her phone to unlock the windows and the door but he'd locked the door to the bedroom where she'd left it on the sill, which doubled as a charging pad. Then, she felt her stomach churn with the first blast of bass. He'd turned on his precious sound system. The one they were (both) still paying off despite her only ever listening to music intravenously podded into her earholes. It lurked in the front room like a malicious machine. The music was some kind of urban garage, fast, pounding, like a power tool. He didn't even like that stuff, he listened to *Dark Side of the Moon* and all that endless, psychedelic, hippie shit. She could feel it through her soles: the walls, the doors, the ironic Venetian chandelier shaking and tinkling. She instinctively went to where the front door handle used to be. It wasn't there. The doors had been changed a few weeks ago. Now they just opened into the wall, sliding with a barely perceptible sigh of air, a little satisfied 'aaah'. It was a smart door. Too smart for a lump of metal-cast handle. What was that anyway? Nineteenth-century technology? Cast brass? Sheesh. There was no way out. She went to the kitchen. Looked for something to smash the glass, took the meat tenderiser out of the drawer and started hitting the window. It barely noticed. The triple-glazing sure kept the heat in well. She kept on hitting. It was beautiful in its way, that hammer. Cast from brass and chromed with decorative details and grooves to let blood run down its shaft. She'd always liked it. It looked a little old fashioned. —**Edwin Heathcote**

THE ETHICULATOR

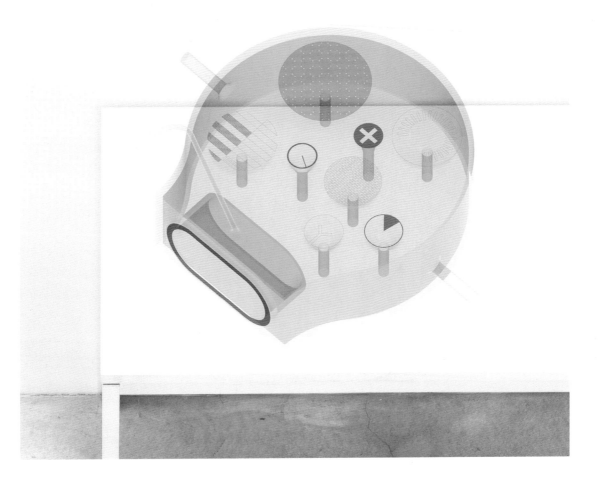

The Ethiculator is a 'smart' device for resolving everyday
ethical dilemmas. This speculative proposal imagines
what the outsourcing of ethical judgment to algorithmic
processes might look like.

Michael Craig-Martin, *Then and Now*, 2017

NEST

Nest Labs, Nest thermostat, 2015.
A Wi-Fi enabled thermostat

GreenScreenRefrigeratorAction aims to give voice to a smart fridge, a device that seemingly has a mind of its own. In a world of 'smart' devices, how might we attempt to understand ways in which technology 'thinks'?

Mark Leckey, *GreenScreenRefrigeratorAction*, 2010

LIVING WITH LESS

With the growth of urban populations in the twentieth century, the question of space became a major preoccupation. From the 1920s onwards, the optimisation of domestic life became a matter of scientific study based on the measurement of the body and the efficient use of space – all of which chimed with modernism's rationalist and functionalist approaches to the home. Less space led to the emergence of hybrid furniture systems – such as the sofa bed, folding tables, mobile walls and integrated storage systems – which served multiple functions. In 1972, Joe Colombo compressed all of the home's domestic needs into a single piece of inhabitable furniture that he called the Total Furnishing Unit. Minimising space and maximising flexibility, it imagined a world in which the home could be reduced to an industrial product made of plastic.

Similar thinking prevails in today's micro-apartments, albeit without the same optimism. High demand for homes in global metropolitan centres is resulting in ever-shrinking living space. Gary Chang's Domestic Transformer apartment in Hong Kong allows for twenty-four different layouts and functions in a single thirty-two-square-metre space. As the value of a square metre increases, so do the solutions that make it bearable to inhabit smaller spaces. Today's micro-living units take the modernist dream of the rationalist home to its extreme. But the creation of smaller units has turned space into a luxury commodity.

What is the absolute minimum to which living space can be reduced? Does squeezing more functionality out of less space help us live better?

Margarete Schütte-Lihotzky, Frankfurt Kitchen, 1926

MINIKITCHEN

Based on detailed studies and interviews with
housewives and women's groups, Schütte-Lihotzky's
modernist kitchen design was the first to consider
contemporary theories of hygiene, efficiency and
workflow. It provided an efficient solution for small
mass-housing apartments.

Joe Colombo, Minikitchen, 1963

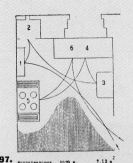

97. Мосгубжилсоюз 1929 г.   т.13 м²

97 и 97 а. Планы обычной
и рационализированной кух-
ни. С т р о й к о м   Р С Ф С Р

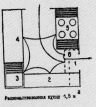

Рационализованная кухня 1,5 м²

97a.

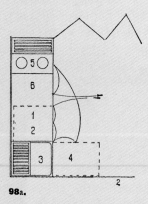

98а.

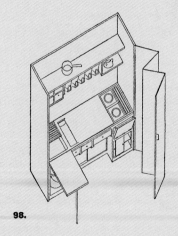

98.

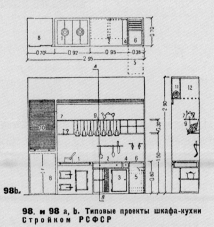

98b.

98. и 98 a, b. Типовые проекты шкафа-кухни
С т р о й к о м   Р С Ф С Р

75

The Narkomfin Building kitchenette had the same width as the Frankfurt Kitchen, but its spatial layout resembled an assembly line. The Narkomfin complex was meant to become a prototype for communal housing, and residents were encouraged to use the shared kitchen. The individual kitchenette would provide an intermediate solution while they adapted to new, communal habits.

Solomon Lisagor, Interior view
of a Type-F unit apartment, c. 1929–33

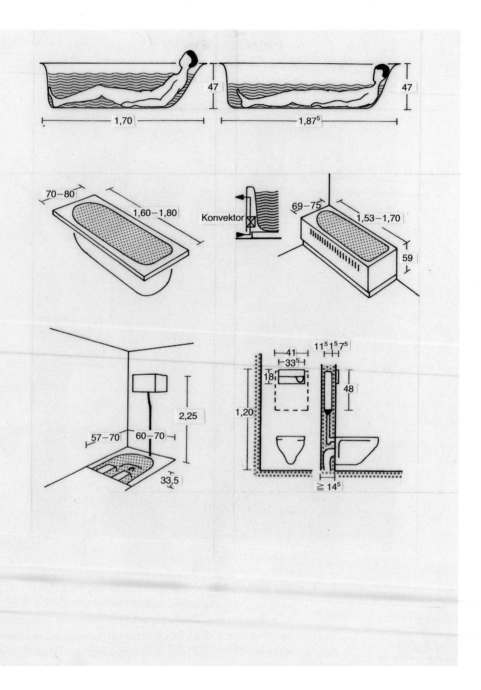

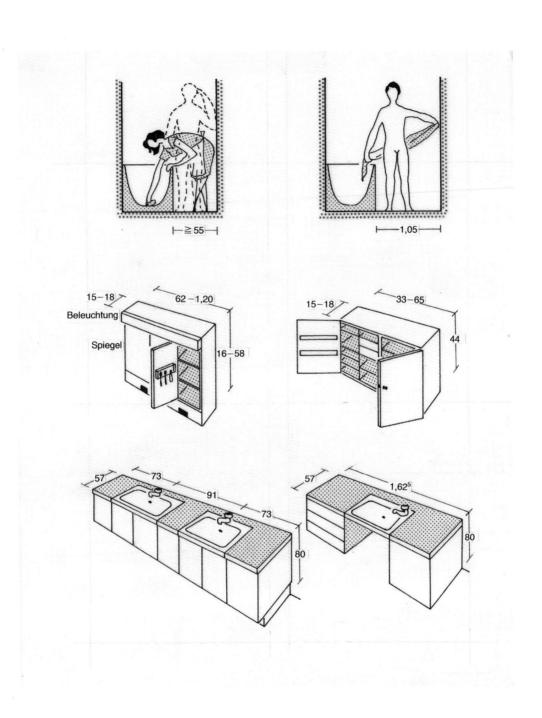

Ernst Neufert, diagrams from *Architects' Data*, 1936.
A handbook for architects and students, containing
numerous diagrams with measurements for,
among other things, the bathtub, sink and cabinets

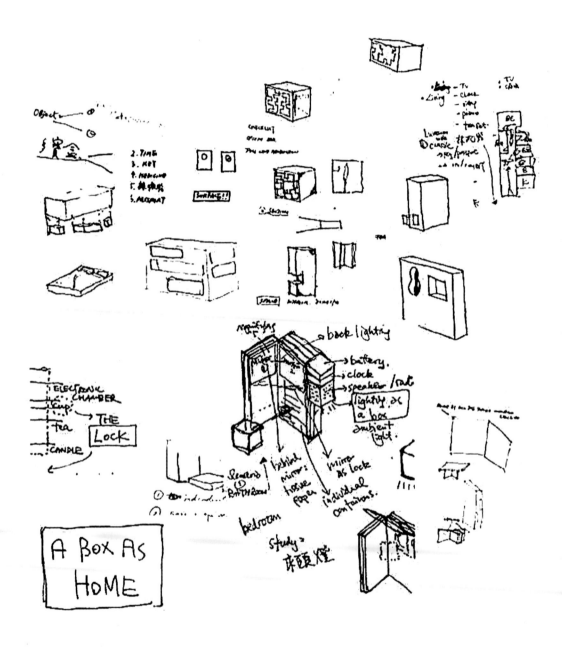

Gary Chang for Alessi, Treasure Box for Urban Nomads drawings, 2007

DOMESTIC TRANSFORMER

Chang built his Domestic Transformer in the same Hong Kong
apartment where he has lived with his parents and three sisters
since his childhood. With its sliding walls, the thirty-two-square-
metre space can be transformed into twenty-four different
rooms. Its luxurious features include a walk-in closet, dining area
for five people, laundry room, a shower and steam room,
and a remote-controlled movie screen that doubles as curtains.

Gary Chang, Domestic Transformer, 2009

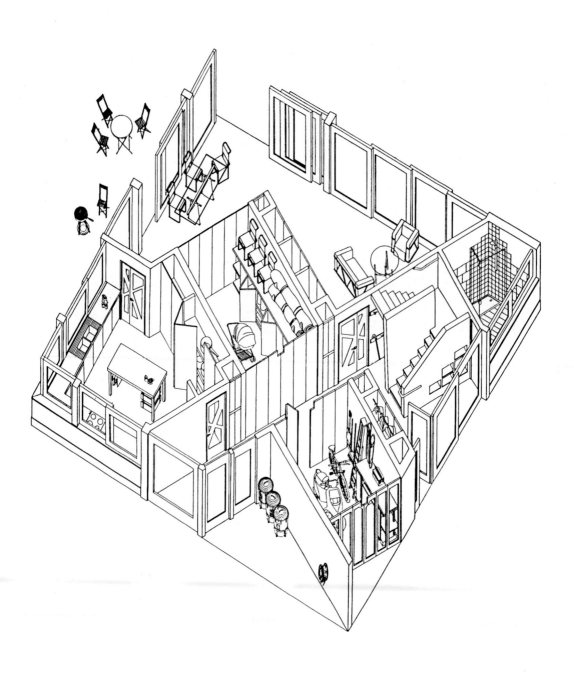

Alison and Peter Smithson, Put Away House axonometric
drawing, 1993, illustrating the ground floor of a building
that is organised around a central storage unit where furniture
and all other domestic possessions can be hidden away

Arthur Rothstein, *Farmers' daughter in storage cellar.*
Fairfield Bench Farms, Montana, 1939

... the pantry?

In the nineteenth century, the so-called 'butler's pantry' was a modestly sized room, placed between the kitchen and the dining room, for storing crockery and other utensils, and where finishing touches were added to dishes before serving. This function did not endure. Modernist concepts like efficiency and space-saving started to reshape the design of the home. Storage space – like the butler's pantry and its lower-income equivalent, the plain 'pantry' – was reduced and integrated into the space of the kitchen. As a result, the total storage of the house – and the kitchen – shrank radically.

These newly equipped and compacted kitchens elicited new ways of storing. For instance, in the USA – and specifically in Manhattan – at the turn of the century, many shopkeepers allowed customers to store food in their large refrigerators. Shoppers continued to buy food in large quantities, collecting it incrementally according to their daily needs. However, shops as shared storage spaces did not last.

Such changes had consequences for our consumption habits. Soon, with less storage space in their homes, shoppers simply began buying less but more often. Sales of canned food grew notably, as did those of pre-cooked products that required reduced storage space and less effort to prepare. Community kitchens started to emerge, offering raw and cooked food on demand. New York is filled with restaurants that offer menus at low enough prices for people to eat out almost every day. A whole world of delivery services have now been launched that aim to mitigate the annoyances of cooking and eating in kitchens with little storage space. These have been boosted exponentially by the development of dedicated apps and online platforms, and have given rise to new urban phenomena such as the emergence of 'ghost kitchens' – popping up in parking lots and other remote places in order to prepare food exclusively for delivery to homes.

The history of the pantry illustrates the indivisibility of the home and the urban macro-economy of food production and consumption. Its disappearance reshaped our daily habits and contributed to the creation of new types of collective spaces. At the same time, the progressive outsourcing of food preparation will probably have an impact not only on how food is produced and consumed in future but also on the contemporary concept of the home and where we draw the boundaries of domestic space. —**Anna Puigjaner**

Joe Colombo, Total Furnishing Unit, 1972.
Installation image from *Italy:
The New Domestic Landscape* at MoMa

TOTAL FURNISHING UNIT

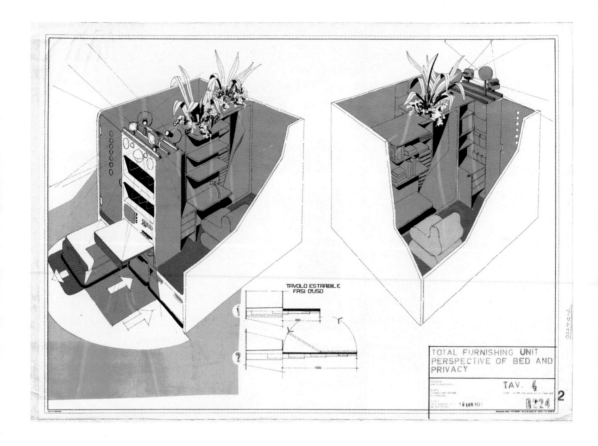

To maximise the potential of small spaces, Joe Colombo's Total Furnishing Unit blurred the boundaries between furniture and architecture. It proposed an inhabitable unit that would flexibly transform and accommodate all the various functions of the home and private life – all within twenty-eight square metres.

Joe Colombo, Total Furnishing Unit drawing, 1972

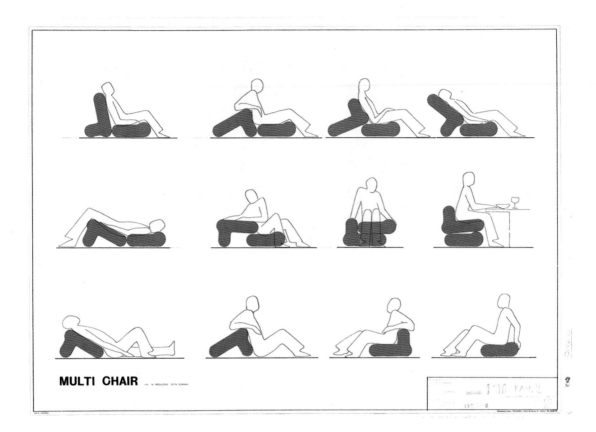

MULTI CHAIR

Joe Colombo, Multi-chair drawings, 1970

Referring to traditions of geometric abstraction
and minimalist sculpture, Zittel's work explores
how we order and inhabit our living spaces

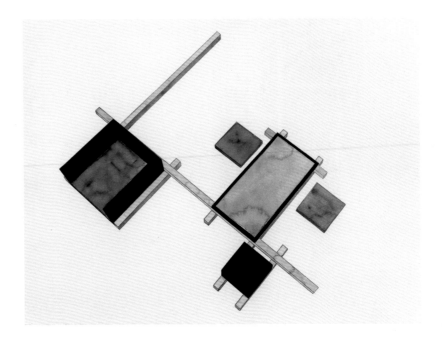

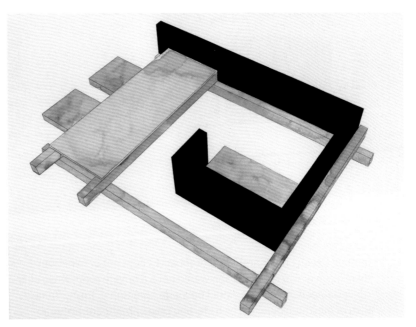

Andrea Zittel, *Untitled*, 2018

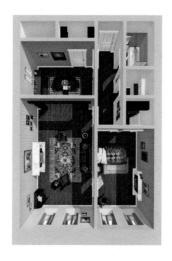

1

2

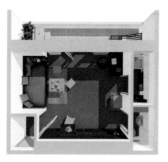

3

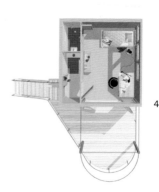

4

In 1932, Czech critic Karel Teige proposed a concept of minimum dwelling in which every person would have a private room while all the other domestic functions would be made communal. Taking Teige's idea of minimum dwelling as a starting point, architectural studio Dogma revisited forty-eight examples of minimum dwelling from the Carthusian monk's cell to the nineteenth-century North American residential hotel, and from the Soviet *dom-kommuna* (communal apartments) to contemporary collective developments.

LOVELESS

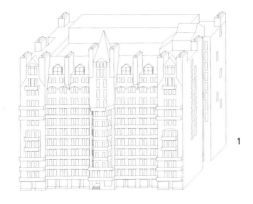
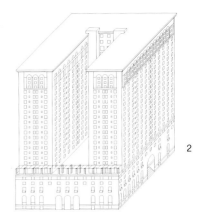
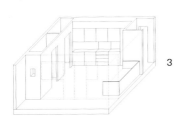
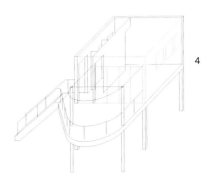

Dogma, Loveless: The Architecture of Minimum Dwelling, 2018

1. Philip G Hubert, Chelsea Hotel Home Club, New York, 1883
2. Warren and Wetmore Architects, Biltmore Hotel, New York, 1913
3. Moisei Ginzburg, Pod House for one person, Moscow, 1930
4. Margarete Schütte-Lihotzky,
One room dwelling for single women, Frankfurt, 1928

The French–Israeli artist Absalon designed six single-occupancy living cells for his own use, which he intended to install in six cities around the world. These minimal structures were made based on the measurements of his own body and his everyday activities such as eating, sleeping, sitting or showering. Painted entirely white, these units would allow the inhabitant to focus on their life without distraction.

Absalon, *Cellule No. 6 (Cell No. 6)* model, 1991

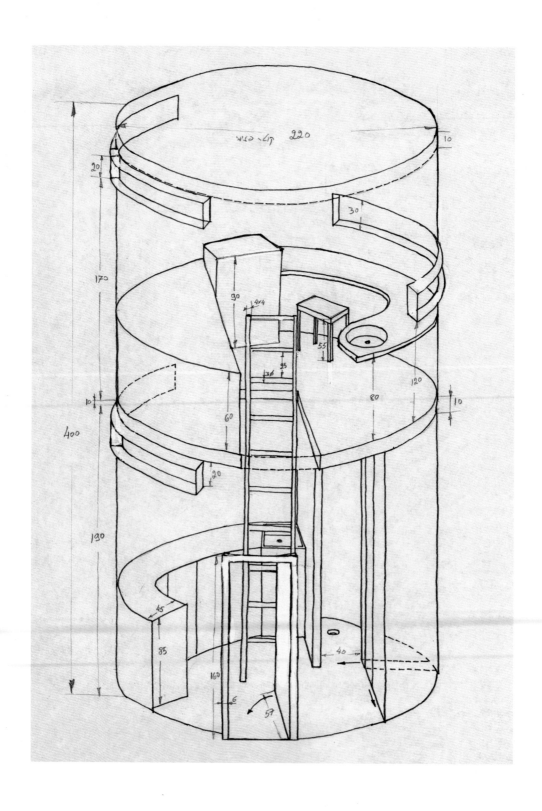

Absalon, *Cellule No. 5 (Cell No. 5)* drawing, 1991

View of the Antique Passage at Castle Howard, 1698

... the corridor?

The word 'corridor' originates not with a space but a person. *Corridore* is Italian for runner, and this etymology suggests an architectural apparatus: a space for moving between rooms. The history of the corridor descends from the houses of the aristocracy, yet, relatively speaking, it is a recent phenomenon. It emerged in Britain in the eighteenth century. Before, in the homes of the powerful, one moved from room to room directly, in a sequence known as 'enfilade'. Progression through these rooms depended on your standing within society.

The phrase 'an Englishman's home is his castle' suggests how everyday dwellings were modelled on the grander homes of the powerful – especially in the Victorian era. The Victorian home was designed as a device that manifested familial, gender, generational and class structures in domestic space. The corridor was a means of separation, an airlock preventing the contamination of each world by another.

It was this highly structured architecture that modernism sought to explode in the early twentieth century. The free plan, which dissolved the separation of spaces, had an ideological as well as an aesthetic agenda, one that reframed domestic space as a more fluid and open field reflecting a more democratic, less hierarchical idea of society.

Through the twentieth century this tendency towards openness has moved from radical exception to ubiquity. Victorian terraced homes were knocked through to connect rooms, loft living arranged domestic space within open frames of industrial buildings, new homes promoted this more open lifestyle in their spatial set-ups: open-plan living in which kitchens flow into dining and living rooms, in which interiors open up to 'outdoor rooms' (aka balconies and terraces). Living imploded into a single continuous space.

We might even argue that the corridor has all but disappeared from domestic life. Today, its only real purpose, as determined by the building regulations, is to provide an escape route – a space that, in the event of a fire, one can run through to safety. —**Sam Jacob**

SOUS LA VIE

Iftach Gazit proposed a way of cooking food in vacuum-sealed bags in the washing machine, using the sous vide cooking method. A speculative project rather than a genuine proposal, Sous La Vie takes the idea of multifunctional home devices to the extreme.

Industrial Facility, Table, Bench, Chair, 2009

LIVING AUTONOMOUSLY

Visions of the good life in the 1970s often involved some form of self-sufficiency, whether making your own furniture or growing your own food. This impulse was fuelled by the desire to escape consumerism, to 'tread lightly on the Earth' and to cultivate one's own abilities. Several designers developed systems that enabled ordinary people to shape their homes with their own hands. Enzo Mari's 1974 *Autoprogettazione* manual demonstrated how to make your own furniture with just some wooden planks and nails, and it remains a classic of 'open-source' design.

Yona Friedman's concept of 'architecture as software' was another attempt to make architecture and design a participatory process. In the 1970s, Friedman collaborated with the United Nations and UNESCO on self-building manuals for African countries, promoting the use of cheap and recyclable materials. Friedman used simple, hand-drawn cartoons to explain his ideas and to remain accessible to those without an architectural or design education.

The internet has made it possible for such systems to reach millions of people. And with the environmental effects of rampant consumerism more evident than ever, there is a renewed desire to find less wasteful ways in which to make, use and reuse domestic objects. As a response to mass-produced furniture, Belgian design studio OpenStructures proposes a modular and open-source system that allows anyone to make furniture and basic household appliances – and then to reuse the parts to make something else. This approach is not only empowering but also reduces waste and saves valuable parts and materials.

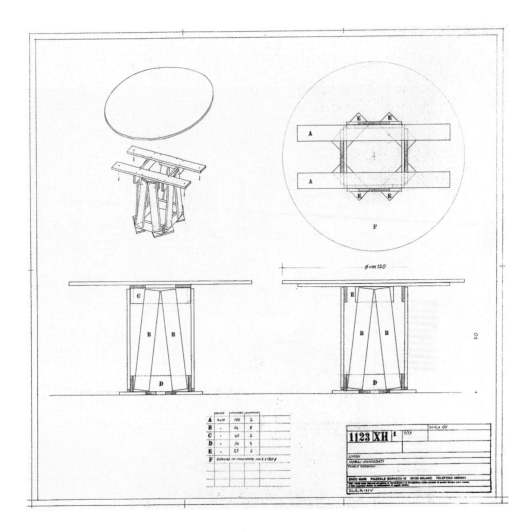

Mari's *Autoprogettazione* manual offered nineteen designs that used timber and required no more than a hammer and some nails to produce. At a time when home furnishings were increasingly becoming an industrially produced commodity, Mari offered to open up the process of design production to the user.

Enzo Mari, *Autoprogettazione*, 1974

Enzo Mari constructing the Sedia chair
from *Autoprogettazione* at its Artek launch, 2010

Jesse Howard, Transparent Tools:
Kettle, 2012

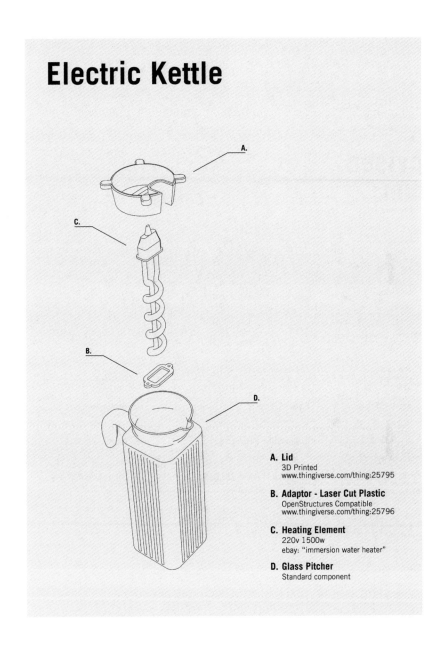

Electric Kettle

A.

C.

B.

D.

A. Lid
3D Printed
www.thingiverse.com/thing:25795

B. Adaptor - Laser Cut Plastic
OpenStructures Compatible
www.thingiverse.com/thing:25796

C. Heating Element
220v 1500w
ebay: "immersion water heater"

D. Glass Pitcher
Standard component

Jesse Howard, production manual for Transparent Tools:
Kettle, 2012. This demonstrates how users
can be actively involved in producing,
repairing and modifying their own products

Improvised
Vacuum

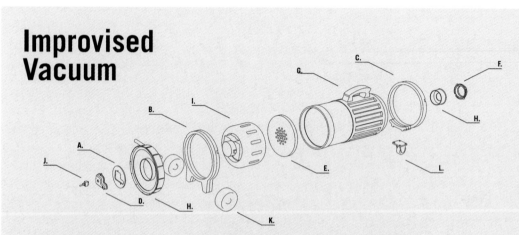

A. Rear Panel - Laser Cut
OpenStrucutres Compatible
thingiverse.com/thing:29923

B. Rear Wheel Support - CNC Milled
OpenStructures Compatible
thingiverse.com/thing:25979

C. Front Wheel Support - CNC Milled
Openstructures Compatible
thingiverse.com/thing:25798

D. Switch Cover - 3D Printed
OpenStructures Compatible
thingiverse.com/thing:25081

E. Chamber Divider - CNC Milled
12mm Multiplex
thingiverse.com/thing:25805

F. Hose Adaptor - 3D Printed
OpenStructures Compatible
thingiverse.com/thing:25802

G. Plastic Thermos Cover
Improvised solution
160mm diameter

H. Plastic Thermos End Caps
Improvised solution

I. AC Motor
Recouperated
from Bosch BSG62023 or similar

J. Toggle Switch
Standard Component
rs-online.com / item# 251-9253

K. Wheels and Axle
Standard Component

L. 35mm Swivel Wheel
Standard Component

Jesse Howard, Transparent Tools:
Vacuum, 2012

Bouré and Mlynčeková for OpenStructures,
OS_things, 2018. A composition of parts to be re-used
in new and imaginative ways to create new objects

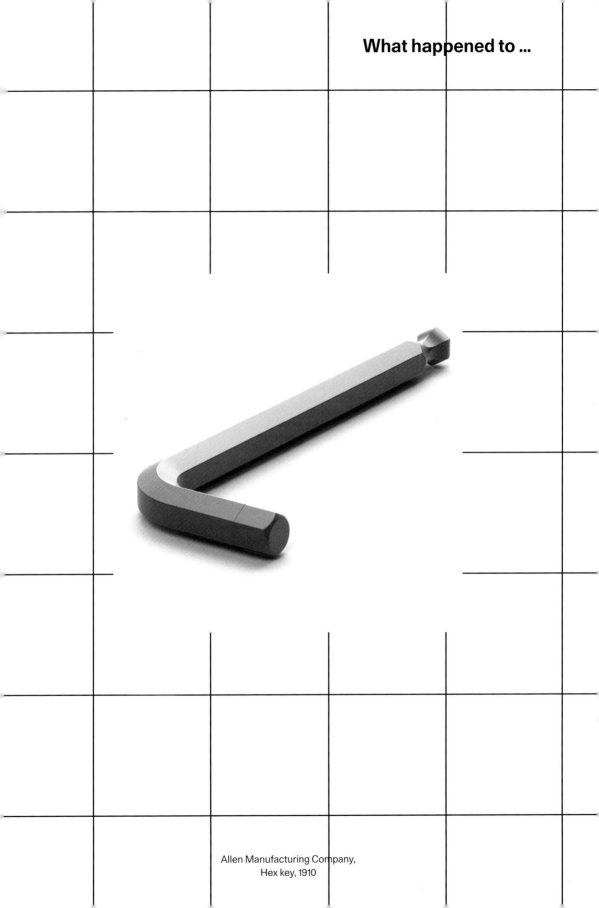

Allen Manufacturing Company,
Hex key, 1910

... the screw?

The screw is a connecting part, an interface. It allows materials to work together. It also facilitates the connection between people by enabling a dialogue through the construction and reconstruction of things. The screw is a globally standardised form. It can be used by anyone, for almost any material, with no need for specialist tools or training. It is democratic. Unlike permanent binds, such as glue, the screw leaves open the possibility of new connections and functions – we don't have to accept already-existing relations and constellations; we can imagine and create different forms and functionalities over time and according to changing needs.

Screws are like worker ants – numerous, anonymous, unappreci- ated. In the past few decades, rather than recognising and celebrating the potential of the screw, we have tried to airbrush it out of existence. Our current society is preoccupied with the façade; it cares only about the surface and prefers to conceal the system, the fits and connections between things. The screw seems to have fallen out of favour as it disrupts our current image of the object as a coherent and perfect whole.

This might explain the move to replace the screw with neat and invisible connections that satisfy our desire for seamless and effortless construction. The promise of ease suggests greater self-sufficiency and further democratisation. But nothing is effortless – the work of connection remains, only now it is hidden from view and beyond our control. Without the screw we remove ourselves from the process of construction and, in doing so, hand control to manufacturers. The price that we pay for apparent efficiency is thus a loss of freedom. Our built environment becomes permanently fixed in a single construction of someone else's design, and we lose the ability and authority to alter it to suit our needs.

Why don't we instead innovate the screw and celebrate the beauty of connection? Otherwise we risk ceding even more control to closed systems: to lose the screw is to diminish our autonomy.
—Christiane Högner and Thomas Lommée

The OpenStructures project explores the possibility of a modular construction model in which everyone designs for everyone and a shared geometrical grid is used to ensure that all components are compatible. The open nature and relative simplicity of these systems means that they have great potential for replication and scalable production. It initiates a collaborative design process to which everybody can contribute parts, components and structures.

Bouré and Mlynčeková for OpenStructures,
OS_things, 2018

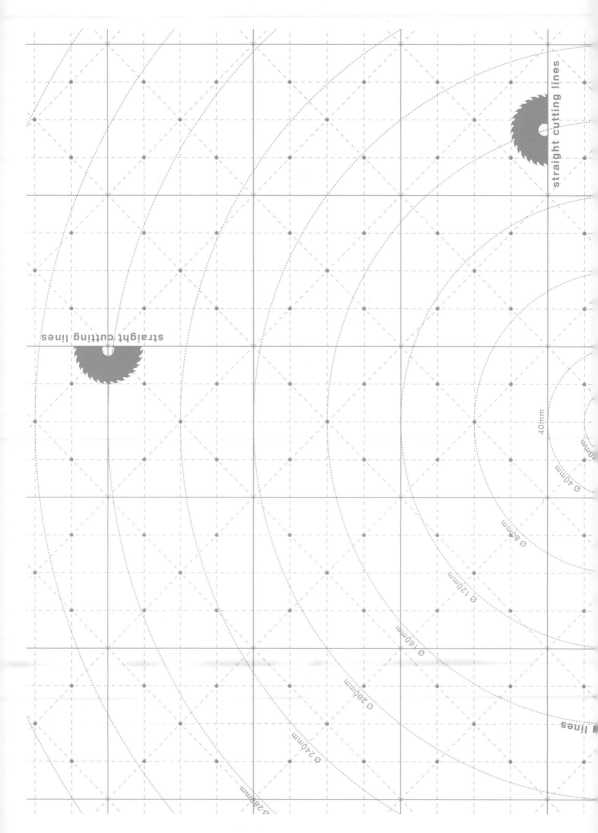

straight cutting lines

straight cutting lines

40mm

Ø 40mm

Ø 80mm

Ø 120mm

Ø 160mm

Ø 200mm

Ø 240mm

Ø 280mm

lines

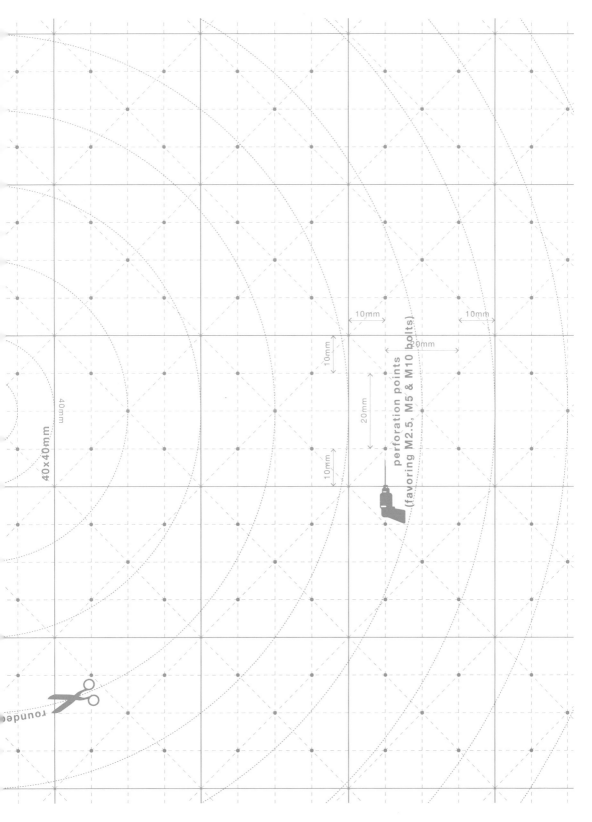

40x40mm

40mm

rounde

10mm

10mm

10mm

10mm

20mm

20mm

perforation points
(favoring M2.5, M5 & M10 bolts)

These 'hacks' are assemblages of parts that
embody new designs and fulfil new functions

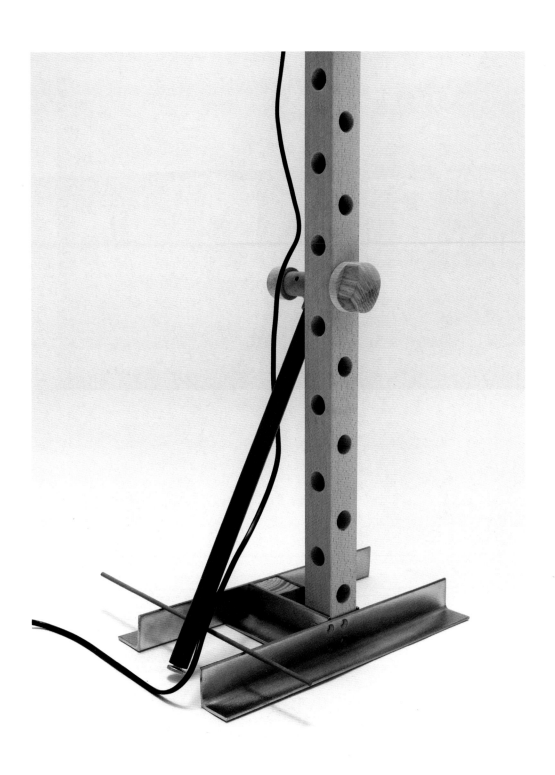

OpenStructures,
Home Futures Hacks, 2018

8' MICROHOUSE

Ken Isaacs, 8' Microhouse, 1972

Ken and Jo Isaacs, Living Cube, 1954

SUPERCHAIR

Ken Isaacs designed modular furniture and housing systems that anyone could build. He published his instructions for how to create a more sustainable, flexible and multi-functional home in the manual *How to Build your own Living Structures* (1974). Isaacs argued that, in the modern world, the process of building is made to seem more complicated than it is. His manuals illustrated how to return to simple construction methods.

Ken Isaacs, Superchair, 1967

Sheng Li Laisi,
R88 cloth tatami bed

... the bed?

Rising house prices and rapidly growing urban populations have forced many people in cities to reduce their living space – a steady retreat from single occupancy, home ownership and private gardens to the flat-share, the bedroom, and, ultimately, the bed. Where once an inhabitant moved between a variety of different rooms with different purposes, the bedroom has now developed into a space for rest, work and leisure.

As high rents make even living rooms a luxury, the bed has become the essential, multipurpose fulcrum of many people's lives. A bed and laptop replace a sofa and television; a bed and some plates, resting on laps, replace a dining table and chairs; social activities that once happened in communal spaces segue from bedroom to bedroom.

Meanwhile, the remote, digital working enabled by the internet – along with the growing casualisation of work – have replaced the traditional office with ... yes, a laptop on the bed. The site of conference calls and late-night emails, the bedroom-as-workplace offers convenience but also isolation and confusion, as homeworkers seek to create boundaries between work life and home life.

Acknowledging today's compact, fluid living conditions, furniture companies have rediscovered an old-fashioned archetype: the daybed. Recalling (ironically) the leisurely comforts of Georgian drawing rooms or Ottoman divans, the daybed is being reissued as the versatile solution to living–working–sleeping on the same spot.

Some prefer more ingenious, transformable solutions to the problem of shrinking domestic space. Low-cost DIY projects and 'hacks' incorporate new functions and concealable units into bedroom furniture. There are also highly mechanised solutions. Ori, an automated living unit created by MIT Media Lab and designer Yves Béhar, allows you to move a wall or conceal the bed at the push of a button.

In the flexible, multipurpose spaces of the contemporary home, the bed can be adapted, enhanced, folded away or displayed as the central, pivotal object upon which most of the day's rituals will take place – which one just depends on what time it is. —**Laura Ridpath**

BIOSPHERE

Yona Friedman, *Biosphere:*
The Global Infrastructure, 2016

SUMMING IT UP
IN A CARTOON

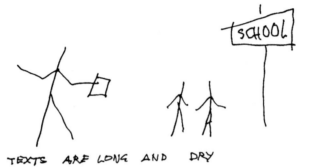

TEXTS ARE LONG AND DRY

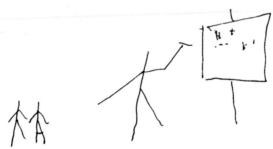

I LIKE TO EXPLAIN THINGS
IN SUBTITLED DRAWINGS

PLEASE, FORGIVE ME THIS WEAKNESS

Yona Friedman, *Biosphere:*
The Global Infrastructure, 2016

IRREGULAR STRUCTURES

MERZ STRUKTUREN

THERE ARE STRUCTURES I CALL "MERZ-STRUKTUREN" AS A HOMMAGE TO THE "MERZBAU" OF KURT SCHWITTERS

THEY ARE CONSTRUCTED FROM ODD PIECES OF ANY MATERIAL: WOOD, METAL, GLASS, CARDBOARD OR PLASTICS

WHICH ARE ASSEMBLED IN WHATEVER WAY THEY CAN FIT

PROVIDED THAT THE STRUCTURE KEEPS UP STANDING

OBVIOUSLY, SUCH STRUCTURES CHARACTERIZE, FIRST OF ALL THE SHANTYTOWNS

WHERE PEOPLE HAVE TO USE, FOR THEIR HOMES, WHATEVER THEY FIND

IN OUR INDUSTRIAL CIVILISATION THE PRODUCT PRODUCED IN THE LARGEST QUANTITY, IS REFUSE, IS INDUSTRIAL FALLOUT

IT IS THE RICHEST RAWMATERIAL OF OUR EPOCH.

WHATEVER YOU WANT TO BUILD YOU CAN FIND MATERIAL FOR IN THE DUSTBINS

IT IS THE MOST PHANTASTIC SHAPES YOU CAN BUILD WITH

SHELTERS,

MONUMENTS

OR SIMPLY EMBELLISHMENTS

YOU CANNOT PLAN, ONLY IMPROVISE

RANDOM COLLECTIONS OF THINGS ASSEMBLED FOR A SPECIFIC GOAL

IS A WAY TO DEFINE "MODERN" (OR WHATEVER) ART

Yona Friedman, *Irregular Structures,*
A Manual, 2005

IMPLICATIONS
IN ARCHITECTURE
FOR A SOFT SOCIETY

CONCERN, FIRST,
WHO MAKES
WHAT DECISIONS

MORALLY IT IS CLEAR:
IT HAS TO BE
THE INHABITANT
TECHNICALLY
THIS IS MORE DIFFICULT

HIS NATURAL METHOD
IS "TRIAL AND ERROR",
WHAT IMPLIES
ULTERIOR
CORRECTIONS

CORRECTIONS
DEMAND TECHNICAL
FACILITY
FOR THE LAYMAN
TO PERFORM.

"TRIAL AND ERROR"
IS POSSIBLE
ONLY IN FULL SCALE
ONLY ON THE SITE
IT IS MORE
THAN A GAME

CORRECTIONS ARE,
IN MOST CASES,
IMPROVISED

(LIKE EVERYTHING
IN LIFE)

IRREGULAR STRUCTURES
ARE THUS MOST
APPROPRIATE

TO CONTINUOUS
CORRECTIONS

EITHER SPOTWISE
IN A COLLECTIVE
FRAMEWORK

OR IN ISOLATED
INDIVIDUAL HOMES

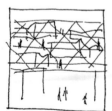

MOBILE ARCHITECTURE
IMPLIES IRREGULAR
RANDOM DISPOSITIONS:

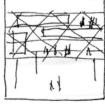

THE ARCHITECTURAL
OBJECT CHANGES
WITH THE INHABITANTS'
LIFE PATTERN

SOCIETY IS NOT A
MECHANISM
BUT A PROCESS

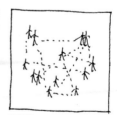

WITH NO FINAL STATE

Yona Friedman's cartoons illustrate how various structures
can be made using odd pieces of any material available

IRREGULAR STRUCTURES

IRREGULAR
STRUCTURES
CAN BE BUILT
EASILY

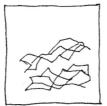

BUT IT IS DIFFICULT
TO DRAW THEM
ON PAPER

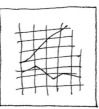

THEY DON'T FOLLOW
RULES
EASY TO FORMULATE

BUT THERE ARE
METHODS
TO BE APPLIED
WHEN BUILDING

IT IS IMPORTANT
THAT SUCH STRUCTURES
DON'T ASK FOR
PRECISION

THEY ADMIT CERTAIN
NEGLIGENCE IN
IMPLEMENTATION,
WHAT THE PROFESSIONAL
WOULD NOT TOLERATE

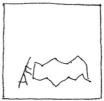

THUS LAYMEN ARE
CAPABLE
TO IMPLEMENT THEM

THESE STRUCTURES
CAN NOT BE SHOWN
COMPLETELY
EVEN IN MODELS

YOU CAN TEST THEM
ONLY IN FULL SCALE

ON THE SITE

IRREGULAR STRUCTURES
ARE OPEN
TO IMPROVISATION

TO CONTINUOUS
CHANGE

THEY HAVE
NO FINAL STATE

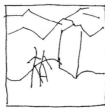

THEY ARE
ONGOING PROCESSES

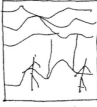

AND OPEN UP
A "SOFT"
ARCHITECTURE

WHICH FITS BEST
A "SOFT" SOCIETY

Yona Friedman, *Irregular Structures,
A Manual*, 2005

Yona Friedman, Merz Structure drawings, 2006

PVC Food Cling Film, 2018

... cling film?

Cling film was introduced to our kitchens at a time when our provisioning, cooking and storage habits were undergoing radical change. The arrival of the refrigerator loosened our reliance on the butcher and grocer, removing the necessity to shop daily for fresh produce. With the fridge we could keep fresh food edible for days and even weeks, and when the freezer arrived that became years. Household fridges became places of abundance, full to bursting with more food than a family could ever eat. Freezers became holders of a family's food security – with a well-stocked freezer a family need fear nothing, rely on no one.

Cling film offered a means of managing this often unruly abundance, trapping the greasy, crumbly, stickiness of food behind a plasticising layer that rendered it smooth to the touch, glossy to the eye. With food's substances and residues contained, cooking and dining came with the new-found promise of 'no mess, no fuss' – a modern way of eating that maximised efficiency and self-sufficiency. Pre-prepared, pre-cooked, pre-packed food offered supreme convenience and ease. Want a three-course meal at your desk during your half-hour lunch break? Just wrap-it-up and pack-it-up. Want to make restaurant-quality food in your home but have no cookery skills? Simply pick up a meal kit with every component thoughtfully pre-portioned, chopped and wrapped in plastic for you to throw together in a pan; no effort required.

It's increasingly clear that this convenience comes at a cost. The no-mess promise of disposable plastics seems like a bad joke when we are confronted with images of the floating islands of plastic in our seas. Where once we pinned the hopes of modernity on plastic's seemingly limitless potential, and aspired to plasticise our lives in Monsanto's *House of the Future*, this admiration has given way to a deep distrust of plastic's shape-shifting nature. The prospect of coating our food in cling film has become distasteful as a fear of food residues has been replaced by a fear of plastic residues in our food and water. Today's responsible parent shuns plastics and fills their kitchen with glass and metal, they wrap their children's sandwiches in recycled wax paper and take their chances with grease marks and spills. Their efforts may be pointless. A study of the umbilical blood of new-born babies found around 200 chemicals in the blood of each. Plastic is part of us now; it's in our blood. —**Mary Miller**

Atelier van Lieshout, AVL-Ville Flag, 2001

Between 2001 and 2002, AVL-Ville was a self-proclaimed
autonomous state founded by Atelier van Lieshout
in the harbour of Rotterdam. It printed its own money;
had its own flag and constitution; and produced its own
food, alcohol and weapons. Balanced between utopia
and dystopia, the project explored the implications of
self-sufficient ways of life.

Atelier van Lieshout, *Autocrat* drawing, 1997

Atelier van Lieshout, *Autocrat*, 1997

Atelier van Lieshout, *Kitchen*, 1998

DOMESTIC ARCADIA

The notion of the 'home of the future' as a machine for living was an attempt to modernise domestic life, but it ignored the human need for ritual. Counter to modernist visions of progress, some designers sought to emphasise that our homes are also places of irrational and emotional needs. Opposing functionalism, alternative ideas of the domestic realm playfully evoked nature. These dream-like, surreal interiors conjured idyllic landscapes, bringing natural forms into the home.

For centuries, designers have imitated and translated natural forms into man-made environments. Frederick Kiesler's Endless House questioned modern architecture's ability to create suitably human habitats. His decades-long project imagined a home made of curved spaces, imitating a 'living organism' inspired by biomorphic forms such as eggs and wombs. In the 1970s, designers working with the Italian furniture producer Gufram used polyurethane to produce natural forms, such as a lounge seat shaped like a giant clump of grass and a coat-hanger cactus. These landscape elements, by turns provocative or poetic, suggest a more primitive, unspoiled existence.

Can the dream of efficiency ever respond to our basic human need for comfort, leisure and recreation? What other ways are there to make our homes better and more fulfilling places to live? This section examines objects that stimulate more emotional or psychological attachments.

Alexander Girard, Metal Wall Relief Sun, 1966

　　　　　Archizoom Associati, Superonda, 1967

Frederick Kiesler, Endless House model, 1958

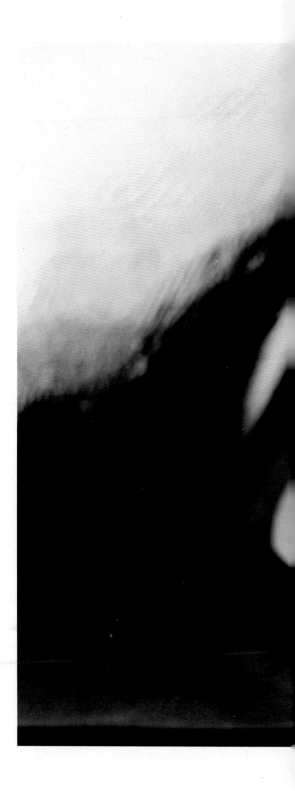

Kiesler's Endless House replaced the rectilinear forms of modern architecture with undulating, curved walls that merged with the floor and ceiling. Kiesler described it as 'endless like the human body – there is no beginning and no end'.

Frederick Kiesler, Endless House model
for Kootz Gallery, 1950

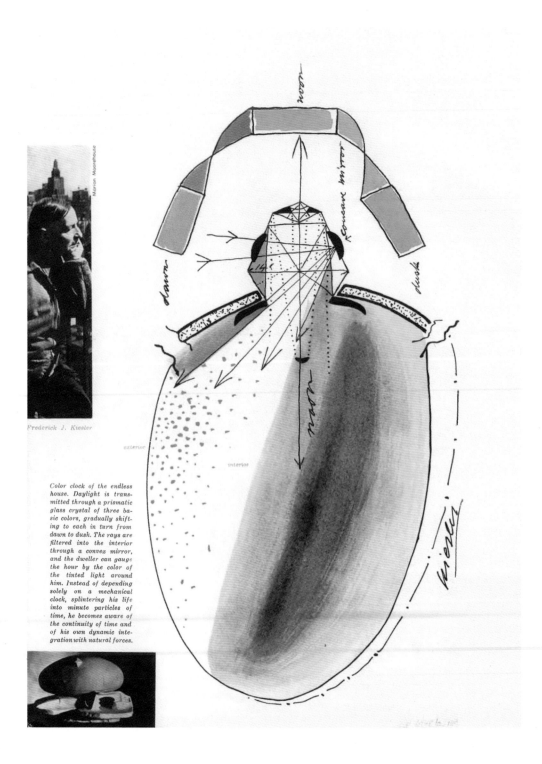

Marion Moorehouse

Frederick J. Kiesler

Color clock of the endless house. Daylight is transmitted through a prismatic glass crystal of three basic colors, gradually shifting to each in turn from dawn to dusk. The rays are filtered into the interior through a convex mirror, and the dweller can gauge the hour by the color of the tinted light around him. Instead of depending solely on a mechanical clock, splintering his life into minute particles of time, he becomes aware of the continuity of time and of his own dynamic integration with natural forces.

Frederick Kiesler, Endless House drawing, 1950

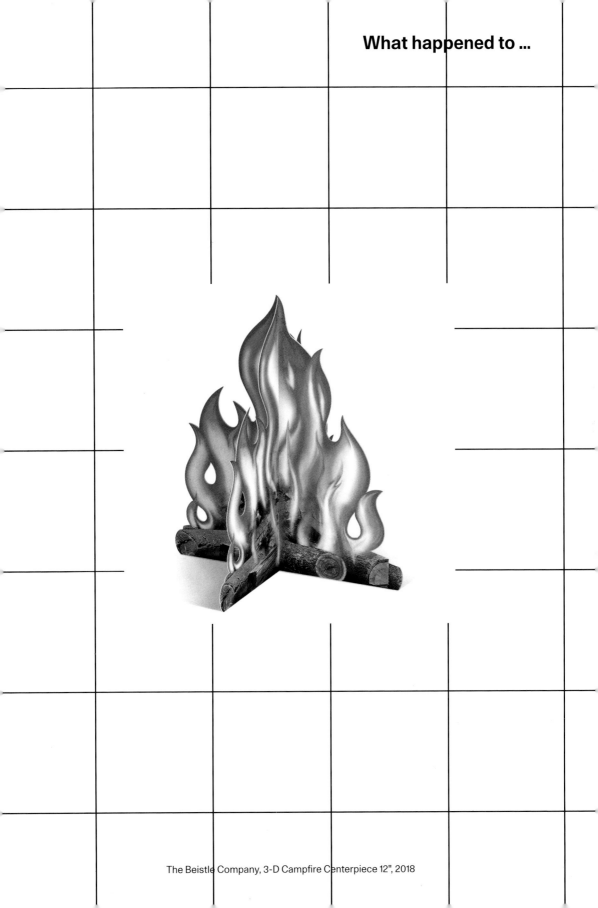

The Beistle Company, 3-D Campfire Centerpiece 12", 2018

... the fire?

The earliest evidence of human-controlled fire dates back more than half a million years. The Wonderwerk Cave in South Africa's Northern Cape Province might be 'the site of the world's oldest barbecue'. Besides cooking, fire also provided warmth and protection. Firelight allowed daytime activities to extend into the evening and warded off night-time predators. This enabled early humans to abandon the treetops in favour of settling and sleeping in caves and on the ground. The control of fire shaped our evolution by fuelling cultural innovation, and dietary and habitual change, as well as the dispersal of *Homo sapiens* across the globe. The fire, contained in the hearth, kept dwellings warm and safe – and so came to define our modern concept of domesticity. Historically, the fireplace was the main source of heat in the house and the place where food was prepared. It was the central location in the home, around which family and guests gathered. Hearth and home were synonymous.

Fire, however, resists control. The 1666 Great Fire of London burned more than two thirds of the city and destroyed many homes. Once the symbol of safety, fire was now recognised as a safety hazard: a dangerous threat to the home and its inhabitants. As the control of open fire inside dwellings became increasingly sophisticated, the fireplace has been gradually replaced by more efficient ways of heating, lighting and cooking. Today, central heating, thermostats, boilers and radiators create an evenly tempered domestic environment.

The presence of the fire in today's homes serves the purposes of nostalgia rather than any real functional use. Think of the candles on romantic dinner tables – or those on birthday cakes, blown out in celebration. Or the fake stuff: electric heaters that mimic the archetypal images and familiar sensations that fire provides; digitised images of flickering light accompanied by a soundtrack of crackling wood. Real fire is now rare in the domestic setting, and therefore a luxury. Take the extravagant AGA cookers that evoke traditional 1920s bourgeois, cast-iron ovens powered by *real* fire. As the numerous celebrity testimonials state in one AGA advertisement, 'No breakfast tastes like the AGA breakfast.' It seems that the fire is back, for the chosen few, and it's here to symbolise a wholesome and luxurious lifestyle: it connects us to the Arcadian origins of the home.
—**Eszter Steierhoffer**

Overleaf
SO-IL's Frame furniture doesn't reveal its function at first
sight, thereby leaving its use open to the imagination.
It seats more than one, if one dares to try. Sitting on
Frame 01 affects the tightness of the mesh, and it changes
the experience of others sitting.

      SO–IL, Frame 01, 2017

Gaetano Pesce for B&B Italia,
Up 5_6 armchair with ottoman, 1969
(reissued 2000)

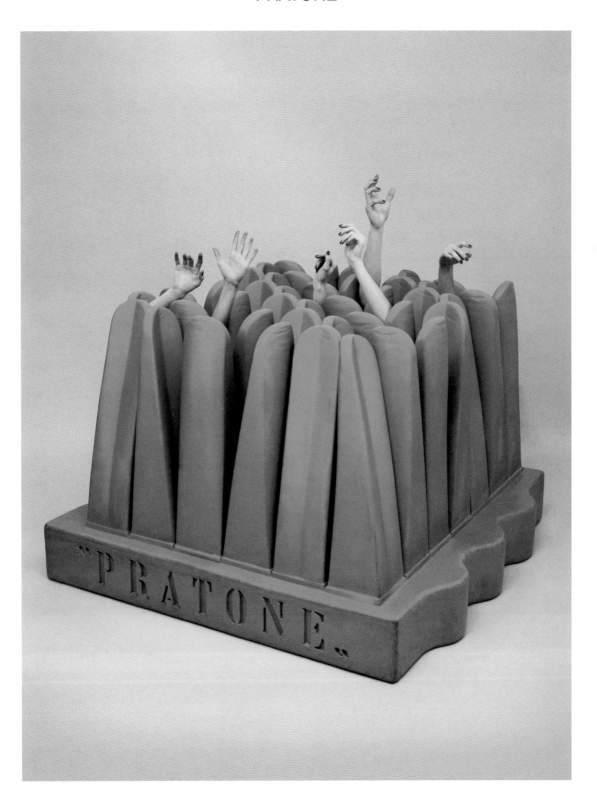

Giorgio Ceretti, Piero Derossi and Riccardo Rosso
for Gufram, Pratone, 1971. A polyurethane lounge
chair resembling a patch of grass

CACTUS

Guido Drocco and Franco Mello for Gufram, Cactus, 1972

Martine Bedin for Memphis, Super, 1981

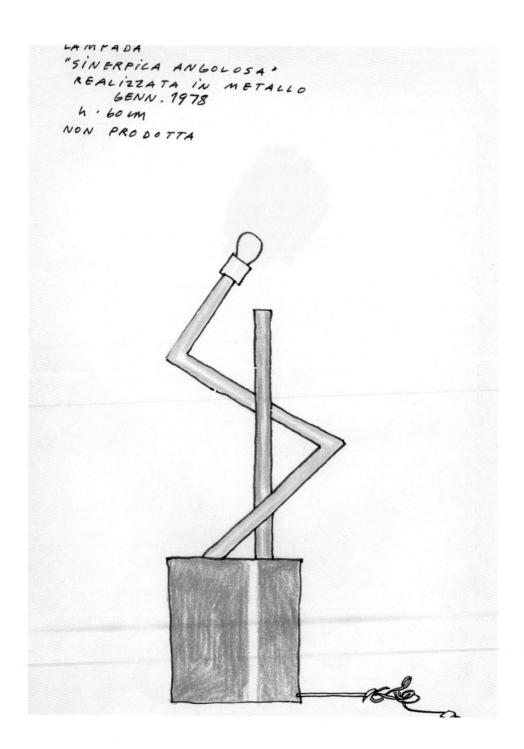

LAMPADA
"SINERPICA ANGOLOSA"
REALIZZATA IN METALLO
GENN. 1978
h · 60 cm
NON PRODOTTA

Michele De Lucchi, Sinerpica Angolosa drawing, 1978.
A table lamp for Studio Alchimia

What happened to ...

Philippe Starck for Kartell, Attila stool, 2000

... the garden gnome?

Who better to room with than the son of Venus and Bacchus? Beyond being a little man with gigantic genitals, Priapus was the god of gardens and fertility. Statues of him have been found in private villas and in the houses of Pompeii and ancient Rome. As such this demigod is considered the forefather of the ornamental hermit or garden gnome, a somewhat peculiar phenomenon that became a craze in eighteenth-century England. A serious country estate would be nothing without a romantic garden, complete with follies and hermit-ages, populated with hermits – fantastical or real. Dressed as druids, these professional recluses would be required to grow their hair and refrain from washing. Yet as the romantic era of 'pleasing melancholy' changed, and the job of hermit disappeared, living hermits gave way to mass-produced ceramic, wooden and, later, plastic garden gnomes.

Although they were popular throughout the twentieth century, it seems that our contemporary culture has let this potent dwarf down. Apart from those fond of kitsch – such as artist Paul McCarthy, who continues to enjoy both the naïve charm and the sexual suggestive-ness of the gnome – the figure has lost its appeal as a room or garden mate. In the East the appetite for outside hooded totems survives, such as Jeju's *dol hareubangs* – penis-shaped rock statues placed in front of gates on this South Korean island, representing gods that offer both protection and fertility. Luckily the internet, in its ability to perpet-ually reverberate with both past and current folly, has helped the Western garden gnome regain some of its stature #gnome-spotting #gnome-napping.

Although the traditional gnome might be gone, sharing one's home or porch with inanimate and fictional figures is as popular as ever. Sony's aibo or Bandai's Tamagotchi – machines that require care in exchange for company – were precursors of the AI-infused pets and robots that will be populating the smart home of the future. As latter-day Snow Whites, we will be commanding seven subservient little helpers to give us massages, scare away fruit thieves or satisfy other needs. But the spirit of the gnome is stoic, mystical and Pan-like. Our modern-day version of this sentiment might be best recognised in the cat; certainly the sheer number of cat videos available on the internet proves that this creature inspires endless amounts of novel, pleasing melancholy. —**Florian Idenburg**

Google's OnHub Makers project invited designers to imagine ways in which an internet router – often shoved under desks or left cluttering hallways – could become the centrepiece of a room. Shells imitating domestic objects such as a fruit bowl or flower vase humanise streamlined forms of technology.

Jenny Wong-Stanley, Helen Levi, Doug Johnston, Bridie Picot, Chiaozza and Katie Stout, Google OnHub Makers project, 2015–18

Ronan & Erwan Bouroullec, Lake drawing, 2018

LAKE

Ronan & Erwan Bouroullec for Vitra, Lake, 2018.
A sofa shaped like a lake that offers
to turn the man-made interior into a landscape

VASE TV

Ronan & Erwan Bouroullec, Vase TV, 2001

ALGUES

A series of designs by the Bouroullec brothers have taken inspiration from the natural world. Algues are a modular system of seaweed-like components that can be connected in an infinite number of combinations to produce a screen, a room divider or a canopy. Easy to assemble and disassemble, Algues is designed for mobile and flexible lifestyles in urban centres.

Ronan & Erwan Bouroullec for Vitra, Algues, 2004

Ronan & Erwan Bouroullec for Vitra, Algues, 2004

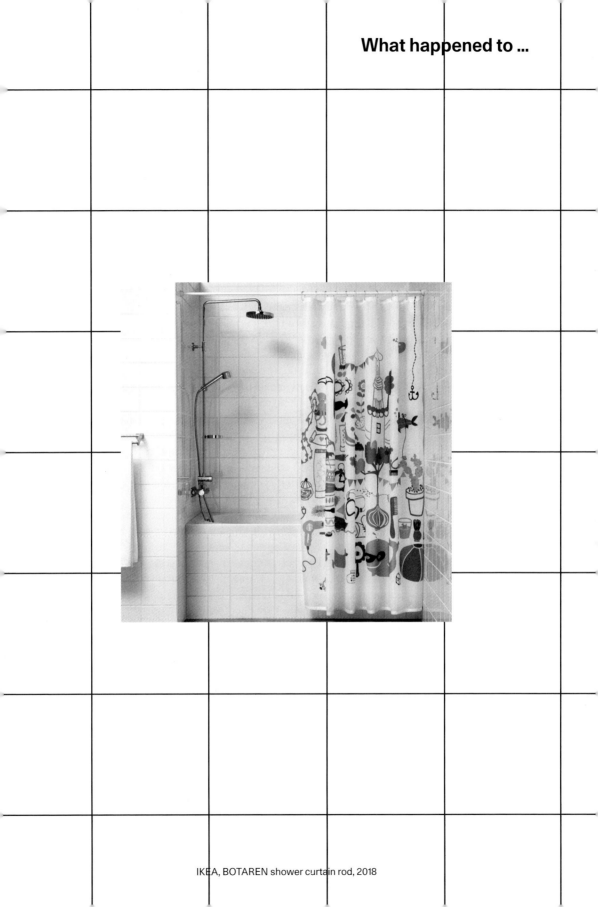

IKEA, BOTAREN shower curtain rod, 2018

... the shower curtain?

Today, bathroom design is aimed at opulence and ease. In a world of heated mirrors (to avoid fogging) and heated floors (to avoid chilly feet) the shower curtain is *persona non grata*. It is a negotiated compromise: it turns a bathtub into a cumbersome and sometimes treacherous shower cubicle. Form follows finance. In a time when expertise is required either to find innovative solutions for shrinking space or to capitalise on the luxurious potential of large bathrooms, the shower curtain has lost its role. It belonged to a different era, one more attuned to improvisations and provisional compromises, where those who liked both showers and baths would have to make do with the shower-bath and its requisite and ad hoc curtain. It could never compete with the solidity of the fixed shower cubicle or the delightfully amorphous space of the wet room.

The shower curtain was often unpleasant: not only did it seem to attract indelible patterns of mildew, it also demonstrated an uncanny magnetism towards bare flesh. In cold bathrooms, the effect of a spray of hot water often created a semi-vacuum, in which cold, dank shower curtains enveloped and clung to showering, cowering bodies. In films, it seemed to attract a salacious misogyny that drew on the erotic potential of the combination of opacity and nudity, and the psychological terror of being so utterly vulnerable. Alfred Hitchcock's *Psycho* captured this tone most completely – not the screeching violins and the endless knife thrusts, but the silent crumpling of the Janet Leigh character's body, clutching the shower curtain for support as the plastic hoops at the top give way one by one.

While the shower curtain seemed to speak of inexpensive utility, it also exhibited idiosyncratic tendencies. Your shower curtain could make it seem as if you were showering deep underwater among brightly coloured fish. It could present your shower as if it were surrounded by gnarled, old wooden doors. It could even, if your humour tended towards the macabre, offer you a version of the *Psycho* shower curtain, with streaks of blood and grim, bloody hand prints.

If in the future we are bereft of shower curtains, it will be because we have moved into a more efficient realm of bathroom fittings that also reflects the disparity between those for whom luxury seems to be taken for granted and those who struggle for necessities.

—Ben Highmore

Michael Beitz, *Divide*, 2010

Andrea Branzi, Animali Domestici
(Domestic Animals) drawing, 1984

Andrea Branzi, Animali Domestici (Domestic Animals), 1985.
A collection of furniture that features natural
materials and resembles creatures and ritual objects,
inviting a new relationship to objects
and a more playful way of inhabiting the home

THE STONES

Piero Gilardi for Gufram, I SASSI (THE STONES), 1973.
Pouffes in the shape of small rocks and stones

TREE TRUNK SOFA

Jurgen Bey, Tree Trunk Sofa, 1999

A modular room divider

Ronan & Erwan Bouroullec, Clouds, 2009

READER

1. T.S. Eliot, *Four Quartets* (Boston, Mass.: Harcourt, 1943).

'Home is where one starts from', wrote TS Eliot, and from there, 'the world becomes stranger, the pattern more complicated'.[1] Insofar as we are constantly shaped by the environment around us, the architecture of the home greatly informs how the self is defined and redefined. Today, as family structures become increasingly varied and the array of ideas of domesticity more diverse than ever, it is an exciting moment at which to investigate the future possibilities of the home.

SO-IL, Breathe – MINI Living, 2017

It might be helpful to begin with a brief history of the house as home. Until not so long ago, the architecture of the home differed significantly from culture to culture. These differences were reflected in the very language used to refer to the home. Italians lived in the *casa*, a structure that holds together; French in the *maison*, a place to remain; Slavs in the *dom*, a consciously built construction; and Chinese in the *wu,* a roof over the head. Each version represented a unique idea of what was to take place in the home and how its inhabitants related to each other. Today, most of us in the so-called 'developed' world live either in a house or in its condensed version, an apartment. Etymologically, the word 'house' is derived from the Old English *hus*, a place that protected people or things, such as grain or livestock, from the elements. People hardly lived in the *hus*. In the seventeenth century, however, Dutch merchants moved into the *huis* and elevated it to a status symbol as they amassed impressive wealth and commodities, which they stored in their domestic space. *Huis* thus became the site for displays of taste and refinement; however, its innate sense as a shelter for possessions remained.

In a typical Dutch *huis*, a compact and often steep staircase acts as the spine of the multistorey building. On each floor, the bedrooms, kitchen, dining room and bathrooms are self-contained and can be closed completely from the adjacent spaces with doors. As a means of storing property, the architecture of the *huis* treated its inhabitants as inanimate objects to be sorted and put away in discrete compartments. It was not its prerogative to participate in the messiness and uncertainty inherent in the everyday. With the rise in productivity during the Industrial Revolution, and the growing demands on work and life, the relative passivity inside the modern-day *huis* – house – provided repose and ease. We found ourselves at home in the house.

The house's passive nature and its primal function as storage also aligned with the double 'wheels' of capitalism: mass production and mass consumption. Thus, the form thrived. We have become increasingly reliant on the objects produced, desired and accumulated inside the house to define a large part of our identities. However, the 2008 financial crisis exposed the fact that the apparent solidity of the house was in fact an illusion. As it was turned into a derivative to be traded in modern-day 'bucket shops', millions of homeowners were ejected from their cosily padded containers overnight, leaving our sense of home exposed and besieged.

Home as a measure of ourselves

Inside the seemingly indifferent walls of the house, however, human relationships continued to transform and become more complex. Destabilised by unprecedented mobility and infiltrated by new technologies, our domestic lives are today full of contradictions, ambiguities and obsolescence. In metropolises such as New York City, people dwelling alone outnumber those living within some kind of family structure. Filling the void of loneliness and the desire to belong, tech giants such as Amazon, Google and Apple are in fierce competition to become an intimate and indispensable partner within our homes. Behind the apparent dependability of new technologies lies the risk of the inhabitant having their agency gradually eroded. Already, we see domesticity as packaged, branded, marketed and sold in a semi-pornographic manner through myriad commercial enterprises such as Airbnb; WeLive; and all-service urban-lifestyle apartments with shared kitchens, a cafe that doubles as a lobby, and on-site pet day care.

Many of the problems with our perception of the home today can be traced back to its origins in the *huis* – in its role as storage, a repository, a thing to be traded. This highly static conception of the home has nothing to offer regarding how we should relate with one another, or with the environment around us. While it encourages personal expression through possessions, it does not do so

2. Kazuo Shinohara, *'Jutaku wa geijutsu de aru'* ('A house is a work of art'), *Shinkenchiku*, vol. 37, no. 1 (Tokyo: January 1962), 77.

through behaviour – and it certainly does not encourage us to try to live uniquely. Other notions of home are more nuanced, more ambiguous, more flexible – but we have lost touch with them. This essay argues that we must try to break free of the house in order to reclaim 'home' as a project that allows us to understand who we really are or who we want to become. This is an idea that we have been pursuing for some time in our architectural practice, SO–IL, but it was through our involvement in this Design Museum exhibition that we began to see more concretely how recent historical precedents might help us to arrive at a different conception for the future of the home.

New orientations and new rituals

Post-war Japanese architect Kazuo Shinohara 'believe[ed] that it will further become possible for the homes we create to offer a total view of what it is to be human'.[2] The weekend home that he designed for the poet Shuntarō Tanikawa in 1974 became a critical point in Japanese architecture shifting its focus towards its own history and tradition. Next to a 'winter house' – which was designed like a pioneer cabin, compact and efficient – Shinohara made a 'summer house' with an inclined, earthen floor, which he called 'the naked space'. In this superfluously large and 'useless' space there is only a sculpture of a rooster, a ladder to nowhere, a single bench and the expressive wooden structure supporting the roof. You might think that the 'naked' quality, as described by the architect, was deployed for ascetic effect. Quite the opposite: by avoiding the functional and logical aspects of the modern house, the architect desired to direct our gaze towards the forest outside through carefully placed windows, the sensorial effects of 'true' materials – wood and soil – and the body's scale in relation to the space. Through this highly curated setting, Shinohara thought that it was possible to recover the interconnectedness that traditional Japanese houses had once enjoyed with the environment in the hope of restoring the Japanese soul, which he felt had been lost in the process of post-war reconstruction.

Kazuo Shinohara, Tanikawa House, 1974

3. Aleksandra Kasuba, 'Tensile Fabric Structures', https://www.kasubaworks.com/live-in-environment.html [Accessed 28 September 2018]

While Shinohara was trying to reclaim a lost sense of home, other designers sought out the sensory in more contemporary terms. Aleksandra Kasuba, a Lithuanian-American artist, built the Live-in-Environment inside her brownstone apartment in New York City between 1971 and 1972, intending to 'abolish the 90-degree angle and introduce a variety of spatial experiences without imitating nature'.[3] Translucent, elastic nylon, a fabric used primarily for military parachutes, was stretched between the ceiling and the floor in fluid lines, resulting in sensuous curves and soft tensions. The artist redrew the generic, rectangular plan of the brownstone with sculptured daylight, layers of translucency and infinite depth of space. Instead of using typical furniture to assign functions to spaces, Kasuba deployed crochet, mohair, mirror, sound and scent to articulate the variety of experiences in each room. What strikes me about Kasuba's house is the way in which she designed around her sensorial needs and, through that, made entirely new spatial qualities seem familiar.

Like Kasuba, the Italian designer Ugo La Pietra asked existential questions about how and where we might live. From the 1960s onwards, his militant, anti-design project Abitare è Essere Ovunque a Casa Propria ('Living is Being at Home Everywhere') illustrated the possibility of appropriating the public realm as domestic space through a collection of makeshift furniture and spontaneous occupations. La Pietra shaved himself in storefront mirrors, hacked an abandoned, plastic street barrier into a sofa and slept in the middle of the street using a portable 'easel' bed. In these ad hoc situations, the home no longer exists within four walls; rather, it can be constructed as a dynamic domestic practice set up between the city and the individual. In resuscitating this relationship and insisting on exchange and negotiation between these two entities, the isolated individual can once again become aware of their intrinsic desire for connection with others and experiment with how that connection can be established. These do-it-yourself, handcrafted objects and instructions broke down the notion that architecture is limited to static and material entities, expanding its context to include the temporal and the ritualistic.

In the Information Age, however, the relationship between ourselves and our environment is much more complex. It can no longer be understood as the simple binary between the individual and the collective. Instead, these two entities constantly reverberate and interfere with each other. Toyo Ito's Pao I (1985) was a proposal for a home for a 'Tokyo Nomad Girl' – played by the young Kazuo Sejima in the photographs – a cosmopolitan young woman who is single and financially self-sufficient. The transparent, dome-like structure offered her no protection from the sensory overload of Tokyo's neon lights and electronic screens – it was a 'naked' form of living, in fact. The Nomad Girl's material possessions are minimal but of symbolic significance. Her space contained a clothing rack, a make-up stand and a mirror.

Aleksandra Kasuba,
The Live-in-Environment,
1971–72

By performing the simple ritual of putting on her make-up in front of the mirror, she sees in the reflection both herself and the city outside. She can see and be seen, as she becomes what the electronic advertisements want her to be. In the Pao, named after the Mongolian tent for nomadic people whose livelihood depends on the natural environment, the Tokyo Nomad Girl fully surrenders herself as part of the design of a new technological world.

Future home today

What should 'home' be in today's world? The idea that we can control the domestic realm simply by alternating between transparent and opaque materials in simple straight lines is becoming obsolete. What is replacing them? At SO–IL we are obsessed with the edge, but one that's not rendered fully transparent as in Pao I. Trespassing, carefully considered as a physical experience, can be rewarding in resuscitating the relationship between here and there, me and you.

In a house designed for the late graphic designer Ivan Chermayeff and playground designer Jane Clark, we made five subtly different glass and stone boxes, each for loosely defined activities. The boxes barely touch each other – and where they touch, you can move from one to another. The textured stone walls are reflected in the glass surfaces, with the boundaries multiplied and the definition of inside and outside almost interchangeable. In another house, perched atop a hill overlooking the Long Island Sound in New York, the mother-of-three's desire for a generous porch was taken to heart. The porch takes the form of *engawa* – covered, outdoor space between interior rooms and exterior gardens in traditional Japanese houses that also functions as circulation. The *engawa* envelops the entire perimeter of the house, and punctures its heart at the crossing in the middle, making ambiguous the idea of whether it's part of the inside or the outside. In the traditional idea of the house, being inside means that one has removed oneself from the environment. But in these projects what is inside and outside is no longer so clear, and our awareness of our exchange between the two is heightened.

What about in urban settings where the environment is man-made – not to mention chaotic, volatile and peopled by neighbours who require endless negotiation? Here, the carefully considered edge might help the resident embrace and even enjoy a healthy dose of instability and disorder inside the home. In the experimental MINI Living tower that we built in an alleyway in Milan, the flexible outer skin was made of a fabric that is light-permeable and breaks down pollutants in the air to be washed off with rain. Inside, the tower eschews a traditional organisation with rooms dedicated to specific functions, forming instead a loose stack of porous realms in which functional elements are paired down to the minimum. The inhabitants sleep on floors that are sometimes netting and sometimes translucent grating padded with cushions. During

Toyo Ito, Pao I: A Dwelling for Tokyo Nomad Girl, 1985

the day, the outer skin is opaque, rendering the tower as a sculpture. At night, it becomes almost transparent as light glows from the inside, like a lantern shining a spotlight on the environment.

The skin, as it transforms throughout the day, establishes a dynamic relationship with its surroundings. Its elasticity and performative nature challenge the idea that containment needs to be enclosure rather than a membrane.

Our lives are pre-organised into master bedrooms, smaller bedrooms, living rooms and kitchens – rooms in which one is supposed to put the TV here and the sofa there. Our habit of compartmentalising and neatly putting away the often messy and conflicting facets of daily life can be undermined by shortcuts and ad hoc elements, creating spaces with ambiguous functions. In a renovation of a typical Brooklyn brownstone, we inserted into the otherwise generic, stacked floors a series of spatial devices that produce serendipitous connections, hybrid functions and surprising discoveries. These include a secret stair leading from the living room to the cellar, a moving curtain track in the library that divides the space in multiple ways, a 'mudroom' with actual mud in it and a skylit laundry room that sneaks into the bedrooms through a closet. These playful and elusive moments promise to draw more dynamic and lively relationships between the various inhabitants of the house.

SO-IL, Breathe – MINI Living, 2017

Once we shed the functionalist approach to the architecture of the home, the sensorial and the ritualistic can come alive again and we might discover that the question of who we really want to become can be rehearsed more consciously as part of the everyday. In my conversation with the artist Janaina Tschäpe about her home and studio, I learned that her kitchen is not merely where food is prepared; it is also heat, sound and smell. Her bathroom is not merely a room with fixtures, but water, view and steam. And her personal studio is not merely where paintings are made, but colour, movement, and retreat. 'We are made to believe that we should rest inside the house, so we can get ready to go out again to do

4. Oscar Wilde, *The Collected Works* (Ware: Wordsworth Editions, 2007), 1104.

things. But we forget that the house can and should also be a place to be productive, without external expectations', said Janaina. By insisting that the architecture of the home be instrumental in the productive and reproductive cycles of human activities, rather than being reduced to an inanimate and acquiescent part of an economic system, we can reclaim the home again for the self.

SO–IL, House in East Marion, 2018

I suspect that the idea of the home of our own time can be found beyond the solid walls of the house and the transparent shell of Ito's Pao I. The more sensuous translucent layers of curved surfaces sketched out by Kasuba express this notion of contemporary domesticity even better. The spatial design that we conceived for the *Home Futures* exhibition strives for a similar effect. When you walk along the soft surfaces, be aware of people on the other side. When you get lost and become unsure if you are browsing in the right sequence, relax: browsing doesn't need a sequence. When you find some corners 'impractical', remember what Oscar Wilde said:

> A practical scheme is either one already in existence, or a scheme that could be carried out under the existing conditions; but it is exactly the existing conditions that one objects to, and any scheme that could accept these conditions is wrong and foolish.[4]

Of all the objects and schemes included in this exhibition, the more impractical ones seem to offer more vitality. As much as they challenge our preconceived notions of domesticity, they also spark new insights about life. The invisible shackles imposed on the home today need to be shaken loose. We can free the home from the functionalist and universal approach to spatial practice. And in our domestic rituals we can imagine an existence more fluidly located in time rather than statically marked out in space. Then, we might truly encounter the future home.

**Pier Vittorio Aureli,
Martino Tattara
and Marson Korbi
of Dogma**

Loveless: a short history of minimum dwelling

The reform of apartments by modern architecture made it
abundantly clear that the problem of minimum dwelling could
not be solved by the mere reduction and simplification
of the floor plan. —Karel Teige, *The Minimum Dwelling*, 1932

1. Karel Teige, *The Minimum Dwelling*, trans. Eric Dluhosch (Cambridge, Mass.: MIT Press, 2002).

2. See Kalus Spechtenhauser and Daniel Weiss, 'Karel Teige and the CIAM: The History of a Troubled Relationship', in *Karel Teige/1900–1951. L'Enfant Terrible of the Czech Modernist Avant-Garde*, eds Eric Dluhosch and Rostislav Svacha (Cambridge, Mass.: MIT Press, 1999), 216–55.

3. Ernst May, 'Das Neue Frankfurt', *Das Neue Frankfurt*, No. 1 (October–November 1926).

4. Various authors, *Die Wohnung für Das Existenzminimum* (Frankfurt am Main: CIAM, 1930).

The idea of 'minimum dwelling' commonly refers to an extremely
reduced space for living, and as such it is associated with typologies such as the micro-flat, the micro-house, the studio-apartment
or even the typical family house reduced to a miniature version.
It was strongly criticised in 1932 by the Czechoslovakian critic and
poet Karel Teige in his book *Nejmensi Byt (The Minimum Dwelling)*.[1]
The book, which focuses on the condition of housing for the
working class, can be read as a critical response to the proceed-
ings of the International Congress of Modern Architecture (CIAM)
held in Frankfurt in 1929, whose topic was 'the dwelling for
minimum subsistence', also known as the *Existenzminimum*.[2]
According to the CIAM architects, *Existenzminimum* addressed
the possibility of solving the housing shortage by reducing dwelling
dimensions to the minimum possible and thus producing a drastic
reduction in building size.[3] To achieve this goal, CIAM published
a compendium of exemplary case studies of housing projects
designed by modern architects that illustrated how houses could
become 'minimum dwellings'.[4] Yet, despite its dramatic reduction,
the CIAM minimum dwelling remained mainly a *family* house –
and it was precisely against the idea of minimum dwelling as
reduction of the typical, bourgeois, single-family unit to a small
house that Teige moved his critique.

Sigfried Giedion and CIAM architects, *Die Wohnung für Das Existenzminimum* (The Dwelling for Minimum Subsistence) diagram, 1930

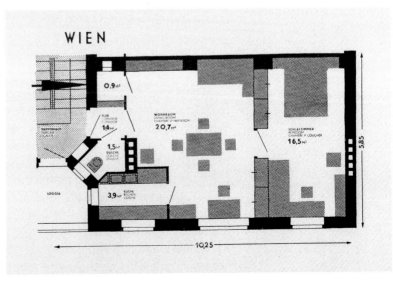

5. Teige, 1–7.

6. Ibid., 17.

For Teige, the CIAM minimum dwelling left unchallenged the essence of housing within the capitalist system: the house as the space that naturalises the patriarchal family structure and thus forms the embodiment of private property.[5] In opposition to the CIAM minimum dwelling, Teige proposed the house as a collective dwelling in which each adult, women and men, would be provided with a 'minimal but adequate independent, habitable room' while all domestic services such as housekeeping, cooking and childcare would be collectivised.[6] This model was not new but inspired by forms of collective living that had proliferated with the rise of industrialisation – such as residential hotels, and boarding and communal houses. Teige understood these precedents dialectically as both extreme forms of the pauperisation of the working class and as a critique of the traditional family household. His idea of collective dwelling was thus an extreme version of these precedents, which he saw as instrumental in changing the habits of dwelling towards an egalitarian society freed from the burdens of domestic labour and private property.

It is thus especially important to return to Teige's critical definition of 'minimum dwelling' as a compass with which to navigate the contemporary, residential landscape of our cities. The ambiguous character of the CIAM proposal, as revealed by Teige's critique, is even more deceptive today when new forms of minimum-living units are often presented under the reassuring image of collectivity, social interaction and sharing. And yet, behind this progressive image, many recent embodiments of the idea of minimum dwelling are again being largely based on traditional ownership structures, on the lack of sharing of domestic chores and on high rental prices, revealing how 'minimum dwelling' can very easily slip between social emancipation and reactionary property speculation.

In the notes that follow, we would like to trace a concise history of the minimum dwelling from its origins to today, following and expanding Teige's critique. Our goal is to show both the contradictions and the potential of the minimum dwelling in reaching a definition of the house not as a private household but as universal, basic space.

The monastic cell and the one-room apartment
Dwelling has always been a collective effort, and yet with the rise of sedentary civilisations the family has established itself as the hegemonic social unit. By 'family', we mean a group of people bound both by kinship and by economic ties, and living in the same place. As such, the family became the quintessential representation of private property in the form of the owner's power over his household as well as over the actual space of his house. It was especially true in the Western context that the house became a physical enclosure separating the household from the rest of the community. It is in this sense that it became a *domestic* space in

7. On the history of monasticism and its relationship to architecture, see the fundamental book by Wolfgang Braunfels, *Monasteries of Western Europe. The Architecture of the Orders* (London: Thames & Hudson, 1972).

8. See Georges Teyssot, 'The Disease of the Domicile', *Assemblage*, No. 6 (June 1988), 72–97.

9. Joseph Connors, 'The One-Room Apartment of Cornelis Meijer', in *Artistic Practices and Cultural Transfer in Early Modern Italy: Essays in Honour of Deborah Howard*, eds Nebahat Avcıoğlu and Allison Sherman (London: Ashgate Publishing, 2015), 45–54; see also Robin Middleton, 'The One-Room Apartment', *AA Files*, No. 4 (July 1983), 60–64.

the etymological meaning of the word. The term 'domestic', which we still use today to address the act of dwelling in the house, comes from *domus*, a Latin word derived from an Ancient Greek term meaning 'to build'. While this etymological origin might seem neutral, the same root gave rise to terms referring to forms of potentially violent control, such as *dominus*, 'the head of the house', and its various declensions: *domination*, *dominion*, and so on. Domestic space is thus always organised around a vector of command that implies a subaltern relationship to power, in which the family is one of the most important institutions.

It is possible to argue that the idea of living apart from the power structure of the family and society emerged in the Middle East in the fourth century AD with the rise of monasticism. While this began as a solitary, 'hermitic' endeavour, it soon developed into communities of peers defined as 'coenobitic', in which dwelling alone was replaced by collective life.[7] It was precisely in reaction to the stress of such collective life that monastic orders like the Camaldolese and later the Carthusians reclaimed the idea of hermitic life but organised as a communitarian pursuit. Their monastic communities invested in the possibility of living together *and* apart, by forming complexes made of self-sufficient one-person 'houses'. As noted by architectural historian Georges Teyssot, this form of monasticism was the seedbed for what would later become a fundamental typology of modernity: the small apartment.[8]

FACCIATA DEL QVARTO MVRO DELLA STANZA.

Cornelis Meijer, One-Room Apartment drawing, 1689

The monastic cell and the monastic housing unit were indeed influential in the development of radically different, modern forms of lodging – from aristocratic, one-room apartments to working-class lodgings and single-person prison cells. One of the earliest examples of secular, solitary living in the city was the one-room apartment designed by the Dutch hydraulic engineer and polymath Cornelis Meijer and published in 1689.[9] This apartment is a room whose enclosing walls are made of built-in furniture

10. Ibid., 'The One-Room apartment', 52.

11. See Rachel Stewart, *The Town House in Georgian London* (London: Yale University Press, 2009), 56.

12. See Wendy Gamber, *The Boarding House in Nineteenth-Century America* (Baltimore, Md: John Hopkins University, 2007).

13. See Dogma + Black Square, *Like a Rolling Stone: Revisiting the Architecture of the Boarding House* (Milan: Black Square, 2016), 22.

that contains everything needed by a gentleman virtuoso – from books to towels, from gold medals to fresh beverages such as wine and spirits. Against the multi-room palace, which entangled residential life within the elaborate rituals of family living, Meijer proposed to compress everything that was needed for a gentleman's life into one space.[10] It was precisely the anxiety of aristocrats feeling the pressure of family ties and the rising bourgeois taste for bachelor life in the eighteenth century that led many of their children to later inhabit smaller, one- or two-room apartments in the city, such as those formed in the townhouses of Georgian London.[11] These townhouses were not communal dwellings but the stacking of independent rooms that shared only essential facilities such as stairs and sometimes a bathroom.

Communal structures

With the rise of metropolitan living in the nineteenth century, single rooms in the form of boarding houses, residential hotels and rooming houses came to represent an increasingly diffuse way of living – especially in the United States, where social mobility and the uprootedness of workers became common features. An early form of such lodgings was the boarding house, where a family would rent rooms to lodgers for a price that included both house-keeping and meals.[12] Often run by women, boarding houses were commercial enterprises that nevertheless advanced a major social revolution in the history of domestic space – namely, the profes-sionalisation of domestic labour.[13] Unlike the family household, in which domestic labour was often unpaid, in the boarding house it was a service provided for a price.

Jean-Baptiste André Godin, Familistère de Guise, 1884

It is interesting to note that this type of lodging emerged at a time when both utopian-socialist movements and feminists were radically questioning the exploitation of domestic labour at home and proposing forms of living that would promote not only the socialisation of cooking and housekeeping but also the parity of sexes within domestic life. As noted by Dolores Hayden, a major source of inspiration for these movements was Charles Fourier's Phalanstère, a communitarian structure inspired by both

14. Dolores Hayden, *The Grand Domestic Revolution. A History of Feminist Design for Homes, Neighborhoods, and Cities*, (Cambridge, Mass.: MIT Press, 1981), 32–53; see also Dolores Hayden, *The Architecture of Communitarian Socialism, 1790–1975* (Cambridge, Mass.: MIT Press, 1976).

15. Ibid., *The Architecture of Communitarian Socialism*, 187–219.

16. See Spencer Klaw, *Without Sin: The Life and Death of the Oneida Community* (London: Penguin, 1994).

17. Paul Groth, *Living Downtown, The History of Residential Hotels in the United States* (Los Angeles, Calif.: University of California Press, 1994), 38.

the monastery and the royal palace, such as Versailles, that could host between 500 and 2,000 people living and working for mutual benefit.[14] Fourier believed that the family household was a major forum of oppression for women, and he conceived the communal life of the Phalanstère to achieve sexual emancipation. Comprising private apartments connected by galleries to a multitude of communal and working spaces, this utopian proposal became extremely influential in the United States, especially among the many socialist-utopian movements that tried to establish self-sufficient communities driven by ideas of social and gender equality.

One of the most interesting applications of Fourierist principles was the Perfectionist Second Mansion House in Oneida, New York state, led by religious visionary and utopian socialist John Humphrey Noyes. The Perfectionists supported complex marriage, which involved a continual change of partners. Among the socialist-utopian communities in the United States, they were perhaps the most radical in dismantling the structure of conjugal love and the nuclear family.[15] In order to support this way of life, the Perfectionists conceived of their home as an array of single rooms connected to a generous amount of communal facilities.[16] The single-person room was not only intended for sleeping but also for contemplation, studying and sexual intercourse. The single room in the Oneida Mansion House is reminiscent of the monastic cell, yet the lack of kitchen and bathroom made clear that this minimum form of dwelling was part of a larger community.

The hotel and the 'home club'

The rise of these forms of living, freed from the burden of domestic life, was paralleled by that of a more commercial and temporary form of collective dwelling: the hotel. As noted by Paul Groth in his important study of hotel living in the United States between 1790 and 1820, associations of wealthy businessmen started to build large structures comprising sleeping rooms and sizable public spaces such as lobbies and restaurants – de facto inventing the modern hotel.[17] A very important archetype of this way of living is represented by the diffusion of the 'palace hotel' in cities like New York and Boston in the nineteenth century. These urban building types, whose appearance resembled the imposing image of a large *palazzo*, boasted centralised housekeeping and a multitude of communal facilities including restaurants and bars, which were often used by residents and visitors as places for working and meeting. This type of living accommodation was suitable for both transient professionals in need of easy but comfortable overnight lodging, and more permanent, wealthy residents who chose this way of life to free themselves from the responsibility of managing large houses and gardens. It is interesting to note that the Palace Hotel in New York hosted not

Philip G Hubert, Chelsea Hotel Home Club, 1883

18. Ibid., 35–36.

19. C Matlack Price, 'A Pioneer in Apartment House Architecture: Memoir on Philip G Hubert's Work', *Architectural Record*, 36 (July 1974), 74–76.

20. Hayden, *Grand Domestic Revolution*, 103–13; see also Dolores Hayden, 'Two Utopian Feminists and Their Campaign for Kitchenless Houses', *Signs* 4/2 (Winter 1978), 274–90.

21. Albert Kimsey Owen, *Integral Co-operation: Its Practical Application* (New York: John W Lovell Company, 1885).

22. Groth, 56–126.

only bachelors but also families who found it convenient to live permanently in hotels, where centralised housekeeping was preferred to maintaining the cohort of servants that would have been necessary in a single-family house.[18]

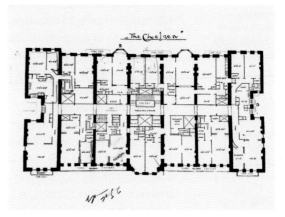

Above
Philip G Hubert, Chelsea Hotel Home Club floorplan, 1885

It was precisely the need to ease domestic life by centralising both housekeeping and food preparation that prompted cooperatives of middle-class families to build so-called 'Home Clubs' such as the Chelsea Hotel in New York, designed by Philip G Hubert in 1883.[19] These clubs represented both a new typology of collective living and a new economic model, in which residents were organised as corporations of shareholders who participated in all aspects of the building process. Hubert's 'Home Clubs' can thus be considered the earliest form of cooperative apartment buildings, and in their earlier incarnations they were called hotels. These cooperative buildings became the inspiration for material feminists such as Marie Howland, who in 1885 developed, in collaboration with civil engineer Albert Kimsey Owen and architect John J Deery, a scheme for an entire city called Tobolobampo.[20] Comprising housing typologies such as residential hotels, collective patio houses and kitchenless family houses, Tobolobampo was conceived by Howland as a 'Hotel City' driven by what Owen described as 'Integral Co-operation', a system in which all domestic chores were socialised and professionally organised.[21]

The 'rooming house'

Around the end of the nineteenth and the beginning of the twentieth century, the United States economy relied heavily on an increasingly mobile population of workers from both middle- and working-class milieux. Faced with the urgent need to provide affordable accommodation to those solitary workers arriving in major United States cities, city authorities, business elites and entrepreneurs strove to expand the formula of hotel living beyond the wealthy classes in the form of 'mid-priced hotels', 'apartment hotels' and 'rooming houses'.[22] While mid-priced hotels replicated in more economic terms the comfort of the palace hotel, and apartment hotels offered one- or two-room accommodation to permanent

23. For a positive outlook on the legacy of Single Room Occupancy (SRO) and hotel life, see Karen A Frank, 'The Single Room Occupancy Hotel: a Rediscovered Housing Type for Single People', in *New Household, New Housing*, eds Karen A Frank and Sherry Ahrentzen (New York: Van Nostrand Reinhold, 1991), 308–30.

24. Chester Hartman with Sarah Carnochan, *City for Sale, The Transformation of San Francisco* (Berkeley, Calif., Los Angeles: University of California Press, 2002), 68.

25. On the rise of the American hotel and the standardisation of architecture, see Lisa Pfueller Davidson, 'Early Twentieth-Century Hotel Architects and the Origins of Standardization', *Journal of Decorative and Propaganda Arts*, Vol. 25, The American Hotel (2005), 72–103.

residents, rooming hotels and houses – also known as 'residential hotels' – provided the most basic form of accommodation possible: a single room, sometimes equipped with a wash basin. All these accommodation types quickly became ubiquitous forms of lodging, and in cities like New York and San Francisco they constituted a major trend in housing provision to the point that there were entire districts, like Fillmore and South of Market in San Francisco, made up almost exclusively of rooming houses for transient lodgers. Apart from the efficiency of their units, all these typologies were devoid of the kitchen and thus had to rely on nearby restaurants. This is the reason that districts with an abundance of hotels also saw a proliferation of stores, bars, restaurants and clubs for association and commercial entertainment.

It is important not to romanticise these forms of minimum dwellings, however, since they were commercial enterprises and therefore marked by strong class division and often racial discrimination. Yet because of their abundance they not only offered cheap and easy accommodation but also gave to many people the possibility to break from family ties, and to reject normative domestic arrangements. Sociologists and historians have emphasised how the proliferation of hotel life in cities like San Francisco was instrumental in the flourishing of countercultural and libertarian movements.[23] Especially during the late 1960s struggles against the urban renewal of districts like South of Market, the lobby space of San Francisco residential hotels such as the Milner Hotel became epicentres of residents' solidarity and bottom-up resistance.[24]

American and Soviet models

From the 1910s onwards the hotel became a consistent architectural type, and there were even architectural firms specialising in its design – such as Warren and Wetmore, the architects of the seminal Biltmore Hotel in New York (c.1913).[25] In this example, we see the classic arrangement of the hotel as podium containing major public spaces and facilities, and supporting a U-shaped tower shaft containing guest rooms with ballrooms at the top floor. What is remarkable about hotels like the Biltmore is how much reduced the size of guest accommodation was compared with those of the nineteenth-century palace hotel, where each room was equipped with a standardised bathroom. At the same time, the smallness of their private rooms was complemented by a generous array of communal spaces and services.

It was, in fact, precisely the efficiency and rationality of the 1920s American standardised hotel that inspired Karel Teige's critique of the minimum dwelling as proposed by CIAM. Yet his embrace of the American residential hotel as the dwelling ideal was also motivated by the way in which hotel life had been appropriated by many Soviet architects in their search for new models

26. Teige, 346–92.

27. Ibid., 334.

28. Ibid., 356.

of domestic living.[26] Teige himself recognised the American hotel as the model that Soviet architects had in mind in approaching the issue of the proletarian dwelling. Indeed, the evolution of the hotel from boarding houses, bachelor flats, dormitories and workers' hostels lay at the origin of the *dom-kommuna,* the Soviet dwelling commune conceived as 'an apartment without private housekeeping functions, a beehive of dwelling cells intended for working individuals'[27] and providing the same housing conditions to everybody, dependent on centralised housekeeping services and complemented by children's crèches, boarding houses and other facilities.

Rather than miniature apartments, as in the nineteenth-century palace-hotel typology, the minimum dwelling was understood by Soviet architects as a series of small, individual cells, each accommodating one adult. Whether the cell was to be used only for sleeping or for other individual activities as well, its dimensions were reduced to the absolute minimum – as in the famous model for the *dom-kommuna* proposed by Mikhail Barsch and Victor Vladimirov in 1929 and used by Teige as an exemplary case of the communal dwelling.[28] Much attention was therefore focused on the minimum acceptable size of the living cells, an amount of surface area that was not too dissimilar to the availability of square metreage per person in Soviet Russia after the end of the First World War but of a completely different quality. It was believed that a dwelling cell of eight to nine square metres within a larger communal structure was capable of offering a higher standard of accommodation than

Moisei Ginzburg,
Individual Pod plans, 1930

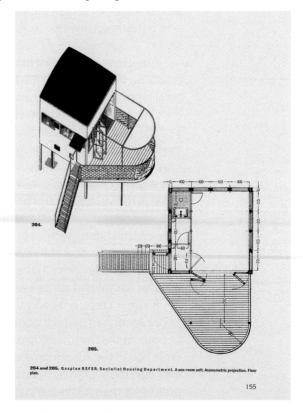

204.

205.

204 and 205. Gosplan RSFSR. Socialist Housing Department. A one-room unit. Axonometric projection. Floor plan.

155

29. Ibid., 346–55.

30. See Alessandro De Magistri, *La città di transizione* ('The transition city') (Turin: Il quadrante, 1988), 37–47.

31. The Strojkom was a committee for the residential architecture of the RSFSR.

32. See Moisei Ginzburg, *Dwelling: Five Years' Work on the Problem of Habitation* (London: Fontanka Publications, 2017), 72–4.

33. On this topic, see also the article published by L Sabsovich in *Sovremennaja Arkitektura (SA)* 3 (1930), 7–9.

34. Ginzburg, *Dwelling*, 148–55.

35. Moisei Ginzburg, 'Abbiamo sentito: Problemi della Tipizzazione dell'Abitazione della Repubblica Federativa Russa' ('We have Heard: Problems of the Typification of the Housing of the Russian Federative Republic') in *SA, Sovremennaja Arkhitectura 1926–1930*, eds Guido Canella and Mario Merigi (Bari: Dedalo, 2007), 234–35.

36. The term 'disurbanism' indicates a series of spatial planning experiments in the early years of the Soviet Union in which settlements were scattered along infrastructure across rural territories. Based on the ideas and writings of Moisei Ginzburg and Michail Ockitovich, the best-known proposal of this approach is Ginzburg and Mikhail Barshch's 'Green City' of 1929.

37. See Marco De Michelis, 'La Città industriale nel Primo Piano Quinquennale' ('The Industrial City in the First Five Year Plan') in *Socialismo, città, architettura URSS 1917* ('Socialism, city, architecture'), ed. Manfredo Tafuri (Rome: Officina, 1976), 156.

that provided by small, dramatically overcrowded, conventional apartments, such as the infamous *kommunalka*, former bourgeois apartments shared by several families.[29]

The concept of communitarian living had been taken into consideration by Soviet architects and authorities since the immediate aftermath of the 1917 Revolution. Yet a systematic approach towards the *dom-kommuna* form of dwelling was adopted only in the 1920s in parallel with the New Economic Policy (NEP), which required a scientific and pragmatic approach to the solution of dwelling in the city.[30] Soviet architects such as those gathering in the OSA (Union of Contemporary Architects) group followed a scientific approach in their design processes, the outcome of which was the development of the first individual cells conceived not as rigid structures but as transitory types for living, which would allow a gradual passage towards the total collectivisation of living. Relevant projects are Moisei Ginzburg's typological experiments for the Strojkom of the RSFSR (Russian Soviet Federative Socialist Republic),[31] including the proposals for the F-Cell type (the model later used in the same architect's Narkomfin building in Moscow) and the E-Cell type.[32]

Deteriorating conditions in Soviet cities in the late 1920s pushed the country's architects towards the 'supercollectivisation' of dwelling. Such an approach was put forward by the economist and urban planner Leonid M Sabsovich in his influential text *The USSR in 15 Years*. In this book Sabsovich posited a scenario in which dwelling was organised through the extreme reduction of the individual living space and the collectivisation of all the other aspects of life.[33] This resulted in the design of large-scale communes housing between 1,000 and 2,000 inhabitants, and city-commune projects in which housing facilities were transformed into dormitories such as the impressive complex of single-person cells proposed as a competition entry for the new city of Autostroj, by a brigade of OSA architects in 1930.

The last phase of the Soviet interpretation of the minimum dwelling is represented by Ginzburg's and sociologist Mikhail Okhitovich's critique of supercollectivisation policies. In 1929–31, they developed a series of prototypes of 'communes' for the Gosplan (state planning committee) of the USSR that attempted to diversify communal dwelling by offering a more nuanced relationship between individual and collective space.[34] The minimum cell, the 'standard unit of soviet residential housing'[35] – as defined by Ginzburg – became the basic unit, which could either stand alone or be part of a larger structure. In this way communal dwelling could potentially accommodate different forms of social organisation – from large, collective houses to the individual pod – and be distributed over 'disurbanist'[36] settlements. Almost nothing of these projects was built and in the 1930s these radical experiments in dwelling were condemned by Soviet authorities.[37]

38. Franco Purini, Eugenio Battisti, Renato Marchini, Antonello Sotgia and Laura Thermes, Al Piano di Sopra ('At The Upper Floor'), proposal for parking-houses for the IACP in Foggia, 1976.

39. For an overview of recent collective-housing projects, see Mateo Kries, Matthias Müller and Daniel Niggli, *Together! The New Architecture of the Collective* (Weil Am Rhein: Vitra Design Museum), 2017.

The new 'minimum dwelling'

While after the Second World War the idea of the 'minimum dwelling' as a theme of architectural research lost the impetus it had had during the previous decade, it has somehow resurfaced in the last few years, stripped of its emancipatory ambition, as a new market product, perfectly fitted to the limited economic possibilities of city dwellers and the profits that skyrocketing property prices in many metropolises guarantee to developers.

A few exceptions exist. These projects were developed in specific historical times, such as during post-war reconstruction or the economic crisis of the 1970s in Italy, for example, when, in a general attempt to address the housing crisis, architects had the chance to develop alternative typologies that were not fitted to the family and were temporary dwellings. Among these, it is worth mentioning Luigi Moretti's Case Albergo in Milan (Hotel Houses, 1948) and Franco Purini's and Laura Thermes' Al Piano di Sopra (literally, 'At the Upper Floor', 1976).[38] Several other design experiments by radical Italian architects centred on the disintegration of the (typical) house as a social unit, such as the Inhabitable Furniture of Archizoom of 1971. More recently, as an answer to the 'precarisation' of life for young workers in large cities, often small-scale and self-organised initiatives have developed in new forms of minimum dwelling intended as the combination of small, individual rooms organised around larger collective spaces, where often both productive and reproductive activities are performed. The Svartlamoen housing in Trondheim, Norway, and the LT Josai by Naruse Inokuma Architects in Nagoya, Japan,[39] represent exemplary attempts to develop affordable dwellings as a way of responding to the disintegration of the family, which has been imposed by contemporary-market labour conditions.

Brendeland & Kristoffersen, Svartlamoen Housing, 2005

Yet, it is undeniable that, with the rise of the welfare state and continuing into the neo-liberal era, the architecture of housing has been dominated by the family dwelling, in the form of the apartment or the family house, making it almost inconceivable today to imagine a 'normal' dwelling not addressing the family. Also, when

40. See Sophie Kleeman, 'Absurd "Co-Living Space" WeLive Is Jacking Up Its Prices', *Gizmodo*, gizmodo.com/absurd-co-living-space-welive-is-jacking-up-its-prices-1789702081 [Accessed 30 August 2018]

41. Patrik Schumacher, 'Only Capitalism Can Solve the Housing Crisis', Adam Smith Institute, www.adamsmith.org/capitalismcansolvethe housingcrisis [Accessed 30 August 2018]

42. See Philippe Van Parijs and Yannick Vanderborght, *Basic Income: A Radical Proposal for a Free Society and Sane Economy* (Cambridge, Mass.: Harvard University Press, 2017); Andrea Fumagalli and Stefano Lucarelli, 'Basic Income and Productivity in Cognitive Capitalism', *Review of Social Economics*, Vol. LXVI/1 (March 2008), 14–37.

Naruse Inokuma Architects, LT Josai, 2013

'minimum dwellings' are produced or advocated for, they tend to be understood as potent speculative tools, capable of extracting profit out of the limited economic possibilities open to today's precarious workers. For example, in cities torn apart by property speculation – such as San Francisco, New York and London – a new version of hotel living is currently being resurrected by companies such as WeLive and The Collective. These firms offer a type of living accommodation that is similar to the old commercial residential hotel but, unlike the latter, pumped up with an overdose of rhetoric about living collectively that masks the very high price of such 'fancy' accommodation (the monthly rent for a studio in a WeLive apartment in New York is around $3,000, if not more).[40] Moreover, these companies target mostly young professionals, the much-celebrated (and much-exploited) 'Millennials', while they exclude people in most urgent need of these types of dwelling, such as disabled and elderly people.

The 'universal room'

In other cases, such as in London, some commentators have recently advocated a new form of housing deregulation that would allow the possibility of offering on the housing market what today would be considered sub-standard living units.[41] All this is clearly far removed from Teige's understanding of 'minimum dwelling' as the possibility of living in common by eliminating the private ownership of the home and socialising domestic labour. The genealogy flowing from Teige's thesis represents for us an invitation to look at this type of home not as the result of austerity measures but as a basic form of living that could be granted to all. In this way, the 'minimum dwelling' can be used to question the role of domestic space as 'private' sphere and envision what could happen if 'home' is no longer a commodity but a universal basic right that can be granted to anyone regardless of class, race, gender and age. This form of 'minimum dwelling' would consist of a generic, average minimum space that, in the same way as the universal basic income proposed by economists such as Philippe Van Parijs and Andrea Fumagalli, aims to support the choice of dwellers to live where and as they want, and to refuse to be part of a specific household.[42] Both the universal basic income and 'universal room' are supposed to be granted unconditionally – and, as such, both policies can be considered a partial reappropriation of capital towards its more even redistribution.

1. Gaston Bachelard,
The Poetics of Space
(Boston, Mass.:
Beacon Press, 1992), 91.

You shut the door behind you. You are home. Your own space, which perhaps you share with one or two others, or with your family. Here you are safe from the gaze of the outside world. Here you can be you. Home is where you can allow yourself to fall into habit, where everything is so familiar that you can dial down your attention, where your senses are not braced for new stimuli. Your own private bubble.

This idea of the home as a private refuge, insulated against the world, is deeply ingrained. You might think it innate to the human experience – a primal instinct, even. Gaston Bachelard, in *The Poetics of Space*, sets out to show 'that a human being likes "to withdraw into his corner", and that it gives him physical pleasure to do so'.[1] You have to remind yourself that, in fact, privacy in domestic life is a relatively recent phenomenon. The private domestic sphere as we currently understand it (since privacy is an ever-shifting concept) is rooted in the rise of the private house in seventeenth-century Europe. However, it is not until the Industrial Revolution, with the separation of work and home, that domesticity takes on its own distinct rituals and expectations. Only in the nineteenth century does privacy become central to the idea of home life. Richard Sennett has linked the rise of privacy to a pair of Victorian sensibilities: one is the protocol of not revealing your inner life in public, and the other is the realisation that children needed sheltering from the modern metropolis. In the growing distinction between the public and private realms, the home came to be the embodiment of privacy.

If the history of domesticity over the last 400 years has seen a gradual accruing of privacy, today it would be easy to argue that we are moving in the opposite direction. This retreat from the sanctity of privacy is being spearheaded by two parallel phenomena. One is a new breed of device that collects your data for the efficient running of your 'smart home'. Smart speakers, thermostats, fridges, light bulbs, plug sockets, door locks, doorbells and vacuum cleaners offer a constellation of voluntary surveillance points. Through these devices, their manufacturers – be it Amazon, Google or iRobot – can learn enough about your home and your habits to, frankly, make you think twice. The second phenomenon is even more voluntary. The confluence of people posting images of their homes on Airbnb and on social-media platforms such as Pinterest and Instagram amounts to an incredible opening up of the interior.

2. Walter Benjamin and Asja Lacis, 'Naples', in *Reflections: Essays, Aphorisms, Autobiographical Writings*, ed. Peter Demetz (New York: Schocken Books, 2007), 167.

3. Peter Sloterdijk, *Foams* ('Spheres' trilogy, vol. III), (Cambridge, Mass.: MIT Press, 2016), 523.

4. Mary Douglas wrote, 'The home protects a person's body from voyeurism' in 'The Idea of a Home: A Kind of Space', *Social Research*, Vol. 58/1 (Spring 1991), 305.

There is no moral judgement here, but there is also no denying that the home has become a theatre of sorts for the performance of our lifestyles.

In their essay on Naples, Walter Benjamin and Asja Lacis famously describe the city's architecture as 'porous' in that it allows so many opportunities for the interior life of buildings to spill out. 'Buildings are used as a popular stage. They are all divided into innumerable, simultaneously animated theatres. Balcony, court-yard, window, gateway, staircase, roof are at the same time stage and boxes.'[2] In these threshold spaces, 'the great panorama' of Neapolitan life is played out. Conversation, argument, song, furniture, utensils – all flood out so that the private seeps into the communal, and vice versa.

This condition of porosity seems apt as a way of understanding privacy and domestic life in the Information Age. The idea that our homes are refuges from others and the outside world, inner sanctums enclosed by solid walls, is one that we may have grown up with but it is increasingly illusory. Our Facebooks posts, our Airbnb listings, our questions to Siri amount to a steady stream of visibility. The home enables the two-way transfer of information in which we demonstrate – sometimes unwittingly, other times performatively – who we are, or at least who we want to be.

Shigeru Ban, Curtain Wall House, 1995

We are perhaps more used to thinking of our homes as bubbles: self-contained micro-worlds, furnished to our tastes, carefully contained behind doors and curtains and revealed only to select acquaintances. No one has made that case more literal than Peter Sloterdijk, who reads the modern apartment as a tiny bubble in a foam of urban dwellers, each sealed off from the other as much as modern technology will allow. But as much as Sloterdijk renders the apartment as hermetically sealed (with its own immune system of climate control and so on), he comes closest to today's reality when he describes it as 'a perfectly insulated egosphere and an easily accessible point in the network of manifold online communi-ties'.[3] In numerous ways, our bubbles are revealed, shared and compared online – they are *content*, visible to audiences that we cannot always restrict. Indeed, while Sloterdijk is only vague about these 'online communities', he is more specific about the smart-home devices that turn your bubble into an interface between commercial services and 'human end consumers'. The bubble, then, is more porous than he maintains.

Does the bubble still ensure privacy? Before we explore just how porous the bubble really is, perhaps we should ask what we mean by 'privacy'. We understand it intuitively as an inalienable right, but one whose edges are never quite clear. One of the functions of home, it seems apparent, is to shield the body from prying eyes.[4] Home meets a psychological need to not feel watched. But traditionally, the distinction between the private and public realms is also linked closely to bodily processes.

5. Hannah Arendt, *The Human Condition* (Chicago, Ill.: University of Chicago Press, 1998), 72.

6. Terence Riley, *The Un-Private House* (New York: MoMA, 1999).

As Hannah Arendt described it, 'from the beginning of history to our own time it has always been the bodily part of human existence that needed to be hidden in privacy, all things connected with the necessity of the life process itself'[5] – which is to say, sex, bodily hygiene and waste. Even in Yevgeny Zamyatin's dystopian novel *We* – which takes place in a city made entirely of glass, where all activities are visible – sex and shitting are screened from view.

Yet such rudimentary interpretations of privacy are hardly sufficient to describe the private realm as we currently see it. Rather, it is a place that we do our best to make in our own image. It is the things we choose to own, the way we arrange them, the way – as Bachelard might say – that we line our nests and our shells, and the fact that this is the one place where we control who enters. Perhaps that rather acquisitive understanding of home is the reason why we consider the tracking of our online purchasing and browsing habits an invasion of privacy. After all, when one is burgled, the most common response is not a pang of loss for the missing possessions but a gnawing discomfort at the idea that one's private space has been violated by strangers.

Despite what I wrote earlier about the history of domesticity being a steady accruing of privacy, there were of course numerous challenges to that in the twentieth century. Modernist architects introduced a degree of transparency to the private home that was unprecedented. The modernists upheld glass and glazing as the culmination of the Enlightenment project, blasting the interior with the light of reason. If such literal transparency was of limited appeal, it was partly because its exemplars were exceptions that proved the rule. Mies's Farnsworth House, for instance, was described by *House Beautiful* in 1953 as 'a glass cage on stilts' – and even the owner, Edith Farnsworth, betrayed a certain discomfort when she described it as 'transparent, like an X-ray'.[6]

In fact, radical transparency was not well suited to the home and ultimately found favour instead in the corporate world with the rise of the glass office building. Here, the transparency of the curtain wall suggested a business ethic that was never literal (more honest was the shift to mirrored glass in postmodern office towers, with their protective opacity). Today, the corporate architecture of privacy is utterly impervious. How telling are the windowless data centres. In these privacy warehouses, where all our metadata is backed up, they have no need for daylight.

Contemporary architects have continued to test the limits of privacy in architectural form. In the mid-1990s, Shigeru Ban made a pun of modernism's love of the curtain wall with his Curtain Wall House: the interior of this Tokyo home could be completely exposed or enclosed by drawing a two-storey curtain around the outside of the building. More recently, Lacaton & Vassal have established a method of expanding existing buildings by wrapping them in glazed winter gardens. There is a suggestion in this strat-

Sou Fujimoto Architects, The Rental Space Tower for House Vision, 2016

egy of the transparent perimeter that what is truly important in a building is its inner life, and that there is no harm or shame in some of this being on display. But the architect who best expresses the complex reality of contemporary privacy is Sou Fujimoto. Through a series of built houses and proposals, he articulates a boundary between the private and public realms that is utterly porous. In his proposal for the *Muji House Vision* exhibition, this is very much along the lines that Benjamin described in Naples, with private rooms opening onto shared balconies, terraces and staircases. In House NA, the home is almost completely transparent and yet is not entirely exposed because it is an accumulation of overlapping glass cells, which preserves some privacy deeper inside the structure. The multi-cellular House NA, despite being a single residence, has the quality of Sloterdijk's foam.

Sou Fujimoto Architects, House NA, 2011

What such architectural strategies are at pains to suggest is that the old dialectic of inside and outside, of public and private, is being replaced by a condition that is much less certain and much more fluid. For most people, however, that is not really an architectural prerogative but a question of information.

The idea that the home is increasingly permeable begins not with the internet and social media but with media itself – the old-fashioned kind. One could trace this phenomenon right back to the arrival of radio in our homes in the 1920s. Already there was the sense, remarked upon by Heidegger and others, that the private realm was no longer completely distinct from the public, as home resounded with signals from the outside world. The advent of television only reified those signals, inviting whole worlds indoors at the flick of a switch. The proliferation of televisual formats led to the inescapable logic – one close to being realised today – that to exist is to be mediated. After all, to most people the words 'Big Brother' conjure up not Orwell's surveillance state but a reality-TV programme in which every mundane action is recorded and thus performed. According to that logic, only those willing to relinquish privacy altogether can be a celebrity. Indeed, the circle of watching

7. Richard Sennett, *The Fall of Public Man* (New York: WW Norton & Company, 2017), 422.

closed with the British reality-TV programme *Gogglebox*, in which viewers watch people watching TV from the viewpoint of the TV itself – here, even the watching becomes a performance.

In the social-media age, those for whom televisual exposure is out of reach (that is, the majority) have other tools at their disposal. Instagram, Twitter and Facebook offer ample opportunity for lifestreaming. And it would be hard to be an assiduous streamer of your life without keeping your hundreds or thousands or millions of followers up to date on the goings-on at home – from renovations to proud purchases, restylings, meals, cats and cacti. Having begun his career writing about the rise of privacy, Richard Sennett must observe with some bemusement its dissolution forty years later. 'In the age of Facebook,' he writes, 'the distinction between public and private is disappearing: intimacies rule the public.'[7]

In 1969, the artist Vito Acconci sought to break down conventional distinctions between the private and public realms. In a work called *Following Piece*, Acconci clandestinely followed a different individual every day for three weeks and wrote a report on their activities. Transgressive and borderline threatening – which is to say, a typical Acconci work – the artist could only follow his targets until they entered a private space, and there the game ended. Today, that is no longer where the game ends – it continues inside. Where being followed was once an intrusion on one's privacy, now we actively seek out followers – the more the merrier – so that we can share our thoughts, our opinions, our holidays, our home and, of course, our lunch. There is even a new class of celebrity that makes its living from being followed, sharing its lifestyles, taste and lunch with millions of people. The members of the Instagram generation put considerable effort into the selective sharing of their lives. This is rather different from the former use of photography to secure precious memories, without thought of an audience. Instead, they live to *perform* their best life. Indeed, the Instagram post has become *proof* of life. 'Pics or it didn't happen', as they say.

Acconci also played this game, in his usual all-or-nothing fashion. The year after *Following Piece*, in a work called *Room Piece*, he transferred the entire contents of his Greenwich Village apartment to the Gain Ground Gallery on the Upper West Side. By making *all* of his private possessions public, he invited the viewer's voyeurism – granted – but one could argue that he also killed it. In the social-media age, voyeurism is selective. No one wants to see *all* of your possessions, the full *catalogue raisonné* of your stuff – what a turn off! They want to see the best stuff, the funny stuff or the cute stuff.

It used to be that only the rich and famous could publish their homes, and mere mortals would fuel their aspirations by leafing through the glossies. Today's aspiring homemaker has Pinterest, and can find handy tips from other mere mortals with enough confidence in their taste to share it with an audience. Pinterest

8. See Alexandra Lange's essay 'Edited Living' in *SQM: The Quantified Home,* ed. Space Caviar (Zurich: Lars Müller, 2014).

boards dedicated to bathrooms, storage solutions or Christmas decorations can amass communities of millions, made up mostly of women.[8] Here, home is constructed through myriad details – there is rarely any sense on Pinterest of the house or apartment as a whole. These algorithmically arranged details facilitate a curious paradox of enabling people to discover their personal taste by emulating others. The idea of the autonomous interior – the true expression of the individual – has been replaced by crowdsourced consensus.

Pinterest, search for 'living room', 2018

If lifestreaming is a form of marketing – the projection of one's personal brand – then it is more literally so when it comes to seizing the opportunities of the 'sharing economy'. Benefiting from Airbnb requires you to publish your home, and to present it in the best possible light. The internet is positively groaning with variations on '20 Airbnb Tips to Make Your Listing Stand Out', pushing 'clean lines' and 'lighting, lighting, lighting'. Again, the marketability of your home mitigates against too much personal expression, as we strive to conform to certain desirable norms. Here the imperative to sell your home as a lifestyle – a not-offputting-ly-unique one – may mean the difference between meeting this month's rent/mortgage payment or not.

Airbnb, Airbnb app, 2018

Of course, there is a difference between the personas that we project online and who we really are. By the same token, some aspects of our home lives – some data – we consciously choose to make public, while others we do not. Which brings us to the final

9. Marshall McLuhan, *The Medium is the Massage: An Inventory of Effects* (San Francisco, Calif.: HardWired, 1996), 12.

10. Ian Bogost, 'Welcome to the Age of Privacy Nihilism', *The Atlantic* (online), 23 August 2018, http://www.theatlantic.com/technology/archive/2018/08/the-age-of-privacy-nihilism-is-here/568198 [Accessed 13 September 2018]

part of this argument that the home has become a porous space: the smart home. The proliferation of connected devices in the home – thermostats, door locks, vacuum cleaners, fridges and speakers, to name a few – completes the home's transformation from a receiver of signals to a transmitter. The 'internet of things' has turned the home into a data-harvesting opportunity with no parallel in human history. And as sinister as that may sound, this is not some Orwellian conspiracy (or not entirely) but simply the new commercial mode by which we pay for certain services with our data. Allowing your Nest thermostat to know whether you are in or out is simply a trade-off for energy efficiency, in the same way that accepting cookies grants you access to an article online. Increasingly, we accept the collection of data for convenience's sake – who has time to read those privacy-protection policies?

So many little red lines have been crossed in the protection of domestic privacy that we are increasingly inured to the data economy and its network effects. So your Roomba robotic vacuum cleaner creates a floor plan of your home that iRobot can sell to other service providers? Well, it beats pushing a hoover around yourself. So your Amazon Echo or Google Home listens to everything you say in anticipation of the trigger word? Well, at least I don't have to put this baby down and type something into a keyboard. One wonders whether future generations will even see such transactions as infringements of privacy. Perhaps what Marshall McLuhan called 'womb-to-tomb surveillance' is simply the price of a frictionless user experience.[9]

Arguably, the real impact of data collection in the home is not the infringement of some notional idea of privacy (one that many people happily waive) but the erosion of our own agency. Because all of the listening, location tracking and purchase logging, all of the Likes and the Shares, coalesce in the ever-improving algorithmic understanding of what you desire. Our data is being weaponised, in the form of targeted advertising, in the name of a commerce so seamless that we no longer have to think about what we want – Amazon will generously relieve you of the burden of choice. This has been called 'privacy nihilism'.[10] That sounds bad, but it's here.

The porous interior, then, takes multiple forms. It is not that the home is merging with the public realm, although that is partially true, but that the private realm is being exposed on several fronts. There are the intimacies that we choose to share in the participative spectator culture of social media. Then there is the data that we don't *really* know we are sharing (which means that we do know but prefer not to think about it), and this we gift to other private entities (corporations) in the name of smooth service. Each form of exposure reflects a type of performance – yours or the device's. And so, as Benjamin might say, the home is both stage and box, where the players and the watchers happily coexist, for now.

Amazon, Echo, 2017

For most of us, home is a great many things. It affords us shelter from the elements, most obviously, but also a platform for conviviality and a container for our earthly possessions. Its address offers us, if we are lucky, a store of social capital to trade on; its walls and spaces, an ark in which familial memory can be borne down through history; and its furnishings a supple, versatile medium in which we might express the uniqueness of the selves we understand ourselves to be.

In recent times, though, the dwelling-place has increasingly been asked to serve one end above all these others. The home is now supposed to support efficiency – not merely its own, but that of its occupants. In sheltering, resting, restoring and entertaining us, it is supposed to underwrite our ongoing ability to act in the world as the autonomous, rational actors the moral–economic theory of our age calls for us to be while expending as little time and effort as possible.

Charles Schridde,
Homes of the Future, 1961

Over the past century, we can see the drive towards efficiency settling over the domestic environment in three broad and overlapping waves, each of them arising in response to the techno-social possibilities of a given moment. The first and longest of these waves, starting around 1920, accompanied the introduction into the home of labour-saving electromechanical appliances – a parade of ever-lighter and more powerful vacuum cleaners, dishwashers, washer/driers, convection ovens and lawn sprinklers, without which the exacting hygienic and self-presentation standards of middle-class existence become hard to maintain.

The second is of far more recent vintage, getting under way only after the smartphone and widespread broadband connectivity had reached ubiquity in the urban centres of the developed world. It translates the distinctively neo-liberal, corporate logic of outsourcing into domestic terms, calving off each distinct function pursued in the course of ordinary household life (laundry; meal preparation; maintenance; even pet-, elder- or childcare) as a task to be mediated by an array of single-purpose apps.

The third, though it found early expression in certain utopian architectural currents of the 1960s and 1970s, is something we can only as yet perceive in vague outline, as a weak signal from a future that may or may not be coming into being. Seeking maximal efficiency by liberating the unencumbered body to dwell and work productively just about anywhere on the planet, this wave of innovation leaves traditional notions of home behind entirely.

Whether framed in such radically nomadic terms, though, or in the relatively drab and conventional ones of an 'Uber for laundry', there is no better way of understanding the trade-offs involved in the quest for domestic efficiency than by pursuing them to their source: the original provision of the middle-class home with labour-saving technological devices, a hundred years ago.

Buckminster Fuller,
Dymaxion House, 1945–6

The automation of home life is a well-trodden path across what is by now a full century of design, but most of the overt celebration of automation as a virtue in itself came during that century's first half. From Buckminster Fuller's Dymaxion House (1945–6) to the Philco-Ford 1999 AD House (1967), there is no trope more central to the era's vision of domestic ease. Most of us of a certain age recognise the exemplary 'Homes of Tomorrow' from a long succession of world's fairs, expos and Walt Disney TV specials. Taking the Corbusian notion of the home as a 'machine for living' with striking literality, these all-electric life-pods pampered their occupants with easy-dusting curves, instant-cooking Radaranges, push-button control panels and hose-down floors.

As little as such Futuramas, Futuros and Houses of the Future (Monsanto or Smithson variety, take your pick) have to do with the way most any of us actually live, or ever will, they constitute much of the loam in which visions of domestic advance are still grown. It's worth attending closely, therefore, to the unspoken and curiously retrograde principle that nestles at the core of all these Homes of Tomorrow, which is that they are intended to afford every class of consumer a level of service previously only available to those with the means to maintain a staff of domestic servants. (This argument was never made more plainly than by a 1924 issue of the French magazine *Je Sais Tout*, an early entrant in the lifestyle genre, which touted a three-storey 'house without servants' in which dozens of futuristic, electrified *appareils pratiques* replaced the butler, the scullery maid, the cook and the nanny.)

Whatever savings of time and energy were realised by such devices were primarily intended to benefit 'the lady of the house', it being assumed by designers almost without exception that the male head of the household was elsewhere, earning a crust. The liberation from drudgery they offered was, in any event, ambiguous and ambivalently received. As Betty Friedan observed in *The Feminine Mystique* (1963), nobody quite knew what to do with the time left over after the daily round of chores had been seen to, and the endless hours in splendid, suburban isolation were every bit as suffocating and soul-deadening for women trapped in the home as the cycle of *métro-boulot-dodo* was for the men tasked with bringing home the bacon. Little surprise, then, that the tranquilliser Miltown (cf. The Rolling Stones' *Mother's Little Helper* of 1966) became the first runaway success of the post-war pharmaceutical industry.

Precisely what was it that the proud owners of these gleaming new labour-saving appurtenances were being freed for? For much of the twentieth century, the canonical answer would have been 'leisure time' – which is to say, a period in which the adult members of the family might amuse, exercise and psychically restore themselves, renewing their labour power while partaking maximally of the fruits of a consumption-oriented economy. Thus, the anticipatory visions of laughing, pipe-smoking dads and gingham-bloused moms so common to the era, waving at Junior through the seamless glass of the swimming pool set into the wall of their living room, or playing canasta in the swivelling, leatherette seats of their self-guiding, bubble-domed futurecars. By mid-century, with the Keynesian economies of the West riding the post-war expansion to heights of collective wealth never scaled before (or, for that matter, at any time since), the architects of domestic tranquillity had seen the future – and it was leisure.

And here we stumble across a problem. After five solid decades of triumphantly unbroken innovation in microelectronics – during which an easy-to-use, global informational network gradually extended until it can reach virtually every domicile on the face of the Earth, and as a parallel revolution unfolded in supply-chain management and low-cost manufacturing – we have never before had cheaper, more powerful labour-saving devices in the domestic environment. A panoply of networked objects is now distributed through the 'smart' home, in a local deployment of what is generally described as the 'internet of things'. In addition to the by-now-unremarkable networked thermostats, light bulbs and webcams, these can include a wide range of embedded sensors and actuators. Increasingly, the white goods themselves are networked, often to no clear end beyond affording the harried householder a remote control in the form of their smartphone, with which to begin the drying cycle or kick on the air conditioner while still stuck in commuter traffic an hour away.

Taken all together, they are capable of optimising the home environment across multiple axes, ensuring that its temperature, lighting levels, security posture and so on all continuously correspond with whatever state is desired by the user. Increasingly, as well, such tasks are mediated via the natural-language speech interface of virtual assistants like Apple's Siri, Amazon's Alexa and Google Home – 'beachheads' in the home for the most advanced consumer-facing artificial-intelligence capabilities that researchers have yet been able to devise. It would seem that peak domestic efficiency is very much within reach of anyone with the nous to download a few apps.

But for all of that, the leisurely future we were promised failed to arrive on schedule. In fact, it didn't materialise at all; if anything, 'leisure' – in the creaky, Affluent Society sense of the word anyway – is a thing that scarcely exists any more. If it isn't the mass production of leisure time, then what problem does the smart home think it's solving? The time saved by going to the trouble of all that continuous modulation is time for what, exactly?

Given that the devices and services in question notably tend to be designed for people whose tastes, preferences and lifeways very much resemble the designers' own, the contemporary Bay Area answer would appear to be 'more code sprints and daily scrums' – i.e. further Stakhanovite exertions on their employers' behalf, directed towards the goal of bringing ever-more-niche information-technological conveniences into being. But there's a strong element of bad faith to all of this as well, and revisiting a curious landmark in the history of automation shows us why.

Recall the curious contrivance that has become known to history as the Mechanical Turk. To the awed delight of its eighteenth-century royal audiences, this seeming automaton played chess at grand-master level, taking on all comers and sending them down to defeat, governed by nothing more than the elaborate assembly of brass gears, cogs and rods visible within its cabinet.

In fact, as we now know, the Turk was cunningly designed to conceal a human operator, and wasn't in any real way automated at all. So many of the tasks launched by a command to Alexa or Siri or Google Home are like this: a desire expressed in a few words, all but literally thoughtless, sends human bodies scurrying behind the scenes to preserve the user's airy sense of automagical effortlessness. (In fact, Amazon has run a distributed digital piece-work service explicitly named Mechanical Turk since 2005, offering what the company too-cleverly-by-half calls 'artificial artificial intelligence' to a global user base, at rates as low as one US cent per task completed.)

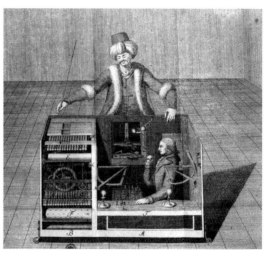

Wolfgang von Kempelen, Mechanical Turk, 1770

If the classic labour-saving appliance, for the most part, did away with the necessity for uniformed household staff by replacing their exertions with electromechanical might, the boomerang twist of the app age is that there are once again human beings in the loop: actual flesh-and-blood servants; merely time-shared, frac-tional ones. Whether the task involves the performance of cleaning and tidying, laundry, grocery shopping, pet and plant care, or light household maintenance and repair, you may be sure that there's an app for that. But the app itself is merely a digital scrim behind which a largely immigrant labour force hustles and sweats and bids against each other, competing for the same jobs. There is inevitably a raced and a gendered aspect to this, as well. If, in the new app economy, the effort and care of household maintenance is displaced not primarily onto machines but onto other bodies, it is notable how often those bodies are female, how very often darker than those requesting the service. The only significant exception here lies in the area of dining at home; a prominent fraction of 'lead users' bizarrely seems to have interpreted the demands on their time as so pressing that they prefer gulping down a flavourless nutrient slurry like Soylent or Huel to a sit-down meal of any kind, even one prepared by someone else.

What we see here is a curious elaboration of something that the educator Bradley Dilger has described as the 'ideology of ease', an implicit (when not entirely open and explicit) body of assertions that undergirds the design of information-technological devices and services, very much including those at the heart of the contemporary home. This ideology proposes that devoting effort or attentional resources to the tasks before us is undesirable – even, somehow, unseemly. Think of it as the demand for convenience raised to the nth degree, articulated virtually as a right.

Accordingly, much of the grandeur in contemporary design lies in streamlining processes until they consist of a few taps at most: the 'Buy Now With 1 Click' imperative. But as a consequence, any opportunity for reflexivity is short-circuited. Whatever values are manifested by these apps, they're folded up like origami inside the interaction flow, no longer available for conscious inspection or consideration. So when you ask Siri to call you a car, that car will invariably be booked via Uber, an enterprise which notoriously refuses to shoulder any of the risk involved in operating a mobility-on-demand service, achieving growth by shedding that burden onto its drivers, its passengers and the communities in which it operates; and when you ask Alexa to order you more dog food, that order will be fulfilled by workers sweltering in a passing-out-hot warehouse where management won't let the doors be opened to admit a little breeze, because of the risk of inventory pilferage; and when you ask Google to book you a table at your favourite restaurant, that reservation will be made via OpenTable, a service that imposes onerous constraints on restaurateurs and waiting staff alike. These allocations of power are subsumed beneath the surface, the judgements and values inscribed in them simultaneously normalised and made to disappear. And if you should happen to find any of this disturbing or offensive ... tough luck. That's just the way things are in smartworld. Effectively, your choices are limited to take it or leave it.

It may have taken us some time, then, but finally perhaps we can learn to see 'smart' for what it so often is: an inscription of power.

For a cohort who experiences even the time spent preparing and enjoying a meal as an intolerable interruption of their availability for work, home life itself is a burden. For them, the very notion of a permanent dwelling is a suboptimal condition – an obstacle to the frictionless mobility our age calls upon us to deliver, and a roadblock on the drive towards total efficiency. And this leads directly to the culmination of this entire line of thinking: the suspicion that the most efficient of all possible homes may very well be no home at all.

Visionary architects of the 1960s believed that the dwelling could be brought with the body, like a shell. This tendency, explored in whimsical projects like Archigram's Suitaloon and Cushicle

(1964–67) and François Dallegret and Reyner Banham's Environment Bubble (1965), reached its apotheosis in Martin Pawley's rather grimmer vision of 'terminal architecture', in which individually scaled mobile shelter units pick their way through the rubbled fields of a blasted transapocalyptic non-scape.

David Greene,
Suitaloon, 1967

A rather more palatable interpretation of nomadism was the 'plug-in lifestyle' foreseen by futurist Alvin Toffler in *Future Shock* (1970), and elaborated in fiction by John Brunner, in the legitimately visionary 1975 novel *The Shockwave Rider*. Brunner's plug-in people went where the jobs were, dipped into casual relationships with whoever happened to be close at hand, moved on from either the moment they stopped being fun, and in any event found the material and human terrain comprehensively prepared for such acts of transience wherever they should happen to alight. Despite a brief enthusiasm for the 'technomadic' life at the moment it first became technically feasible, though, around the turn of the millennium, the Toffler/Brunner vision seemed unlikely to win adoption at scale.

But things have changed in the years since, with the rise of the network and the cloud; the ubiquitous provision of smartphones to serve as interface and mechanism of payment; and, not least, the stunning global spread of Airbnb, whose success supports the business case for the new wave of co-working/co-living ventures. Finally the logic of outsourcing can be raised to its perfect realisation. You can now offload virtually all of the processes that underwrite domestic life onto a commercial service provider, allowing you to focus on your core competency, whatever that should happen to be, and to pursue it wherever on Earth you are able to find an audience, a market or a community.

At present, there is no suggestion that anything beyond the tiniest number of people will ever choose to live this way full-time. But it would be unwise to count it out completely. Consider WeLive, a residential offering developed by the hugely successful WeWork chain of co-working spaces, which orients its offering towards

1. David Greene, '# Great speculations /// Living pod by David Greene', *The funambulist*, thefunambulist. net/architectural-projects/ great-speculations-living- pod-by-david-greene [Accessed 10 September 2018]

WeWork, WeLife app, 2018

a customer base that is 'always working or always semi-working'. Or Roam, a competing 'global community of coliving and coworking spaces' that offers members the opportunity to touch down and get busy at their San Francisco, London, Bali, Miami or Tokyo locations, for prices starting at $500 a week.

Such propositions clearly gesture towards some of the more fantastic archi-social visions of the late 1960s and early 1970s – the ones in which hip nomads roamed planet-spanning super-surfaces and megastructural interiors *ad libitum*, equipped with no more than a *cache-sexe*, a small pouch for personal effects and perhaps a cloak against the acid rain. If you squint hard, you can make out the last, tattered remnants of that imaginary in the existing real-world global archipelago of short-term flats and co-working spaces, knitted together by ubiquitous broadband connectivity and low-cost flights, and undergirded by other, rather less glamorous enabling infrastructures (chiefly extended-stay motels and self-serve storage-locker chains). It is possible to bounce around the nodes of this network for years on end, and indeed there are some who seem profoundly fulfilled by the years they spend doing so. Here we drift intriguingly close to, again, Archigram: 'the need for a house (in the form of a permanent static container) as part of [human] psychological make-up will disappear.'[1]

It isn't so much that the plug-in vision of unlimited freedom was superseded, or even betrayed, as that its present-day realisation for a few reveals something telling about what the rest of us want and need. For all the implicit value placed on liberation in the de-homing movement, just the opposite appears to be happening – reflecting a need most of us have for continuity and stability at a time when very little else seems to be holding fast.

But for some tinkering around the edges – primarily driven by the micro-home ventures of the real-estate industry, and perhaps some experimentation with household structure on the part of those embarked upon polyamory – the twenty-first-century home remains astonishingly conservative. In its stasis it offers a place to recover from the world, perhaps even from the pressure towards efficiency itself.

In our time, this is no longer a matter of Taylorist time-and-motion studies or Dreyfusian calibrations of the body in space but something more intimate still – harder to define, and far less concrete. It's about reforging yourself to meet the demands of a brutally competitive market for your labour: making yourself fit, rested, ready, reliable, available via multiple communication channels at any time of day or night, and ready to go wherever the work takes you. Seen in this harsh light, even cultural trends that are entirely unobjectionable on their face – the turn towards minimalism, say, or the rise of streaming services, or the Kondoesque pursuit of decluttering – can be understood as moves toward frictionlessness and the elimination of anything that would encumber the home-dweller as plausible service provider and autonomous economic actor.

Superstudio, *Supersurface, The Happy Island*, 1971

As we've also seen, the pressures involved in supporting this way of life cascade downwards to a frankly subaltern class, who are exposed to many of the same requirements of personality, fitness and perpetual availability as the middle-class home-dweller and actor in the knowledge economy, yet expected to tolerate the whims, tantrums and outright harrassment of their betters in silence. The question, then, remains today what it always has been: efficiency for whom, exactly? Whose time and energy are valued, and whose are sacrificed on the altar of another's freedom to move and to act? If we but trace it with a little care, the new logic of domestic ease makes the answers to questions like these distressingly, unavoidably clear – to the point that whenever any such proposition arises, it's worth interrogating both its 'smart' and 'home' aspects with the greatest care.

Sarah Kember　　**Sexing the smart home**

1. Genevieve Bell and Joseph Kaye, 'Designing Technology for Domestic Spaces: A Kitchen Manifesto', *Gastronomica* (Spring 2002), 46–62.

The smart home is a vision, a futuristic fantasy, a partial reality, a set of prototypes, a way of inhabiting the 'internet of things', a science and a fiction, a means of promoting branded technologies, a revisionist form of Artificial Intelligence ('smart is the new AI'), a way of regulating space and time, and a mechanism for reproducing domestic roles and identities.

What is most striking about the smart home of today is its resemblance to the future home of the past. Making that connection, comparing twenty-first-century and twentieth-century visions, doing a history of the future is important because it puts futuristic ideas in context. It reminds us that our visions of tomorrow are always deferred, and tell us more about the values of the present than the designs of times to come.[1]

This essay examines the values associated with home and the reasons why our projections seem to have changed so little. It asks why Microsoft's prototype looks so much like Monsanto's of the 1950s, and brings a feminist perspective to bear on the reappearance of 'Mrs Housewife' in futuristic kitchens full of the latest technologies.

Back to the future

The RCA Whirlpool Miracle Kitchen was a travelling exhibit and showcase for American technological progress and politics in the late 1950s. An inventory of the devices on display reveals the extent to which the technologies were – and remain – inseparable from

Whirlpool Corporation, RCA Whirlpool Miracle Kitchen, 1959

2. Ruth Oldenziel and Karin Zachmann, 'Kitchens as Technology and Politics: An Introduction', in *Cold War Kitchen. Americanization, Technology, and European Users*, eds Ruth Oldenziel and Karin Zachmann (Cambridge, Mass.: MIT Press, 2009).

3. Frederick Winslow Taylor, *Principles of Scientific Management* (New York: Harper & Brothers Publishers, 1911).

4. Robert Kanigel, *The One Best Way: Frederick Winslow Taylor and the Enigma of Efficiency* (New York: Penguin, 1999), 7.

5. Ibid.

Richard Nixon and Nikita Khrushchev's 'Kitchen Debate' at the American National Exhibition in Moscow, 1959

the politics. The demonstration revolves around a militaristic planning, or mission-control, centre. From here, the homemaker, who of course is female (and white and middle-class and, needless to say, heterosexual), has push-button access to security cameras, television screens, temperature and lighting control, and a host of automated cookers and cleaners including a robot floor-sweeper and a weird, self-propelled serving trolley.

The manufacturers were not selling a real kitchen, as the technologies did not yet exist. So what were they selling? And to whom? One answer, of course, is the American way of life as opposed to the Soviet way of life. Consumer capitalism versus communism. The contest centred on technological progress and prowess – on the arms race; the space race; and, quite literally, on the kitchen of the future.

During a temporary thaw in the Cold War, the Soviets agreed to host a United States exhibition in Moscow during July 1959. Here, Nixon and Khrushchev met and quarrelled over displays such as the Miracle Kitchen, turning what was subsequently dubbed the 'Cold War kitchen' into a locus of ideological differences.[2]

One of the defining differences concerned the importance of efficiency in the development of industry and in the development of the home of tomorrow. Derived from Frederick Winslow Taylor's *Principles of Scientific Management*,[3] the idea of efficiency 'so permeates the soil of modern life we no longer realize it's there'.[4] It is Taylor who gives us, to this day, an 'unholy obsession with time', order, optimization and productivity. We live with his vision of a 'clockwork world of tasks timed to the hundredth of a minute' and of standardised machines and standardised men and women who use them.[5]

Taylorist kitchens, however, saved time and made time for women. Labour-saving technologies created leisure time. Automated dishwashers and self-cleaning ovens meant, in the 1950s, more time for bridge, or tennis lessons or coffee mornings. That was the idea. That was the claim. It was not the reality,

6. Ruth Schwartz Cowan, *More Work for Mother: The Ironies of Technology from the Open Hearth to the Microwave* (New York: Basic Books, 1985).

7. *Design for Dreaming* (1956). Directed by William Beaudine. USA: MPO Productions. Initial release 1 April 1956. www.youtube.com/ watch?v=4_ccAf82RQ8 [Accessed 8 September 2018]

8. *Groundhog Day* (1993). Directed by Harold Ramis. USA: Columbia Pictures. Initial release 7 May 1993.

as numerous feminists have argued. The future homemaker of yesterday had to operate mission control, excel at sport, be sociable and still get meals made for the family. Who would maintain this newly sterile, factory-like environment of the home? More technologies make more work for mother.[6]

'Déjà vu all over again'

Flashback to 1956, and a film made by General Motors entitled *Design for Dreaming*.[7] In fact, it's a musical – and it starts when a Prince Charming character, resembling Fred Astaire in a mask, enters a woman's bedroom. He has come to invite her to the 'ball', otherwise known as the Motorola exhibit, featuring the latest GM cars. Our Cinderella is given a gown and literally swept off her feet, flying out of the window to the show. 'What would you like me to buy you honey?' he asks, and she says she wants them all: the Corvette, the Pontiac, etc. Suddenly, she suffers a wardrobe malfunction. 'Hey lady, your apron is showing', shouts one helpful spectator. 'Better get her to the kitchen quick', offers another. Cinderella is duly carted back to the kitchen: 'Just like a man: you give him a break, and you wind up in the kitchen baking a cake.' Fair point – except that this is, of course, a kitchen like no other: 'No need for the bride to feel tragic, the rest is just push-button magic.' This is a newly automated, labour-saving kitchen, so 'whether you bake or broil or stew, the Frigidaire kitchen does it all for you'. This is a Taylorist kitchen that saves time and makes time for women. Cinders is liberated: 'Tick tock, tick tock, I'm free to have fun around the clock.'

MPO Productions and General Motors, *Design for Dreaming* film still, 1956

The film has a happy ending. Cinders, transformed back into a princess, returns to the show with her Prince Charming and they drive off in a Firebird 2 along the highway of tomorrow into a future where our dreams come true. So what happened to that future? Did our dreams come true? Think déjà vu or *Groundhog Day*.[8] We're still having the same dream.

The original promotional video for Microsoft's prototype smart home (1999) puts Janet back in the kitchen quick. As far as I know,

9. Betty Friedan, *The Feminine Mystique* (London: Penguin Books, 2010).

10. Quote from 'Cinderella' in *Design for Dreaming* (see note 7).

11. www.youtube.com/ watch?v=DoCCO3GKqWY [Accessed 8 September 2018]

she never got to go to the ball at all. But she does have a kitchen like no other. It's smart, so it can talk to her. It says, 'Janet, would you like some help with your baking?' and she says yes. She puts a bag of flour on a hotspot on the kitchen worktop and a recipe (for focaccia bread) magically appears. If you watch carefully, you'll see the same thing happen in the Miracle Kitchen demonstration. Then, the cameras in the ceiling scan the Radio Frequency Identification Device (RFID), a tag on Janet's medicine bottle, and remind her when to take her pills. 'Janet,' says her worktop, 'don't forget to take your medication.'

Microsoft, *Smart Home* film still, 2000

What is that about? Betty Friedan, in *The Feminine Mystique*, talks about the psychological cost, the mental distress and the subsequent medication of women who were part of the workforce when men were at war but then returned to the home and to traditional gender roles in the post-war period.[9] In order to understand why a similar process of re-domestication and re-traditionalisation might be happening now, it is important to recognise a certain dynamic here: a process of both promoting and containing progress. While the progress of technology is promoted, political progress is contained. What happened in the 1950s is happening today; a focus on the domestic realm is helping to anchor traditional gender roles and hierarchies at a historical juncture when the absorption of feminism and other progressive movements into mainstream politics – and, indeed, when technology opens up and challenges conventional roles, identities and possibilities. A return to the home, and specifically to the kitchen, is a way of making the future safe: 'Everyone says the future is strange, but I have the feeling some things won't change.'[10] Indeed.

Plastic, plastic everywhere

The film promoting Monsanto's prototype *House of the Future* (1957) is presented by their plastics division.[11] The first five minutes or so is particularly interesting. The film speaks of a revolution so quiet that it had, so far, gone unnoticed: the introduction of vinyl flooring, melamine countertops, styrene tiling, plastic-based paints and so on into homes all across the United States. However, in order to support further research and development, the industry

12. Ezio Manzini, *The Material of Invention. Materials and Design* (Cambridge, Mass.: The MIT Press, 1989).

needed to publicise itself, to get across the message that plastic was both functional and decorative. It decided to demonstrate its disruptive potential and mount 'a dramatic attack'. Plans were drawn up for an 'idea with three dimensions', an exhibition house that would showcase all of the uses for plastic and present a 'statement of what could be done with the first truly manmade material'.

As the film progresses, we see a family walk inside the newly constructed, futuristic space located in the Tomorrowland section of a Disney theme park. Father makes for the front room where the gramophone is. Mother and daughter enter the kitchen, and mother experiences a wardrobe transformation as she dreams of making dinner in a space composed of plastic flooring; plastic ceiling panels; plastic dishes; a plastic table; and seemingly plastic, but in actual fact irradiated, food: 'design and science combined for the utmost convenience and food preservation'.

Monsanto, *House of the Future*, 1957

Plastic was an innovation that needed to be promoted through the development of consumer products, but its disruptive or revolutionary potential was as much contained as it was displayed in the home. As Ezio Manzini argues in *The Material of Invention*, all materials acquire cultural values and communicative habits through use and becoming part of the syntax of design.[12] In the 1950s, we knew that stone was durable, wool was warm and steel was cold. We did not know what plastic was. It had no identity and it now symbolises materials that have no identity, that are 'plastic' in that they are malleable, versatile and ambiguous. Western cultures are uneasy with ambiguity, although, of course, with climate change and growing concerns about waste – especially the build-up of plastics in the world's oceans – it is likely that plastic has now passed the baton of ambiguity to another material and become, finally, identifiable as bad: an environmental ill. During the 1950s, the association between plastic commodities in the home and women returned from the workplace to the home was a way of managing the ambiguity of material and gender alike.

13. Bell and Kaye.

14. www.youtube.com/
watch?v=wk146eGRUtl
[Accessed 8 September 2018]

15. Sarah Kember, *iMedia.
The Gendering of Objects,
Environments and Smart
Materials* (Basingstoke:
Palgrave Macmillan, 2016), 47.

16. Ibid.

17. Isobel Armstrong, *Victorian
Glassworlds: Glass Culture
and the Imagination 1830–1880*
(Oxford: Oxford University
Press, 2008), 6.

The *House of the Future* exhibition marked a turning point between homes as spaces for living and houses as stages for the performance of technologies and materials of the future.[13] A popular attraction between 1957 and 1967, it brought in 5–10,000 visitors a day. Located in a theme park, it was oriented as much toward entertainment and popular-media consumption as it was toward scientific and technological progress. Always mediated and on display, the house of the future, from this point on, is, paradoxically, designed for mass consumption but not for real habitation.

Glass is the new plastic

Corning's *A Day Made of Glass* (2011) is a viral YouTube video.[14] It stars Jennifer, who, like the protagonist in *Design for Dreaming*, is asleep in bed. She gets up and goes to the bathroom where her information-enabled mirror opens five separate windows: live news, weather, temperature, automated applications (including shower settings and coffee maker) and today's schedule. Jennifer has an executive brief, a project meeting with production and a brainstorming session with the team, all before 10.00 a.m. She gets a notice that her 9.30 meeting is now at 8.30 and, by touching the 'ARCHITECTURAL DISPLAY GLASS. Pristine Surface, Electronics Enabling, Touch Sensitive', she is able to confirm.[15]

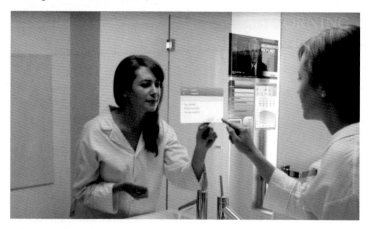

Corning, *A Day Made
of Glass* film still, 2011

Smart glass is not just tinted glass, able to switch from transparent to translucent. It is glass embedded with information technology. Contemporary manufacturers, including Corning, are promoting smart glass in the home where women such as Jennifer and Microsoft's Janet are confronted with to-do lists and schedules that appear in windows; screens; and, very often, mirrors. Mirrors reflect the preferred subject of the future home, one who is still obsessed with time, order, efficiency and productivity; one who saves time and makes time; and one who undergoes a mythical process of transformation, Cinderella style.[16]

Glass is, of course, the founding element of the Cinderella story, the glass slipper functioning as a magical product: the agent of a transformation from scullery maid to princess (and back again).[17] Glass is an old material as well as a magical one. It retains its identity – clear, transparent – even as that identity is morphed by its newer, more plastic, more elastic, more organic properties, through which glass is becoming itself transformed into a kind of intelligent skin. Smart glass is an interface between interior and exterior worlds. It is becoming thin and flexible, elastic like skin and even warm to the touch. It wraps around devices, giving them their double – visual and tactile – lustre, and it wraps around us: our cities, homes and bodies. It is becoming increasingly ambiguous, a shape-shifter: a grotesque.

In Corning's video, Jennifer never gets to the office. She is returned to the home via a shopping trip for clothes, modelled, in glass, by rotating, three-dimensional avatars.

Smart sexism

Let's be clear about the gender politics here. Corning's Jennifer is shopping, trying on her appliqué ruffle blouse in the mirror. Where, in the meantime, is her husband? He is conducting virtual brain surgery in his 'WALL-FORMAT DISPLAY GLASS. Durable, Seamless, Wall-Size Coverage, Touch Sensitive.' Back at home, she is in the front room, having an extracurricular astronomy lesson with the kids while he lies in bed, reading HG Wells's *The Time Machine* on his 'PORTABLE DISPLAY GLASS. Ultra Thin, Flexible, Electronics Enabling.'

Futurism has always been a masculine as well as a tech-driven affair, despite early and ongoing feminist interventions. Composition of the World Future Society is predominantly male. The statistics, around seventy to eighty per cent, are the same in the tech indus-try, in which women are still confined to communication roles and excluded from areas such as programming. Women are capable of gender bias themselves, of course, and part of the problem is that programmers and engineers are not trained to think about technology in a cultural context. Cultural agnosticism is a way of designing in cultural bias. We end up with an array of possible futures that are, at the same time, unaware of, and delimited by, the historical conditions from which they emerge.

Driven by innovation, and solutions-oriented, the smart tech industry is not so much providing solutions to existing social problems as coming up with solutions in need of a problem. This is one way of explaining Microsoft's smart bra, complete with a heart monitor and skin sensors, measuring the signs of stress and designed to prevent stress-related overeating. It may not be an adequate explanation for Ravijour's chastity bra, which, as its name suggests, remains firmly locked until the wearer's heart rate reaches a level pseudo-scientifically associated with true love, whereupon, hey presto, the thing flies off. Ironic and nostalgic forms of sexism are still sexism.

The smart home is a locus for wearable and environmental technologies, embedded in everyday materials and objects, becoming increasingly pervasive and harder to perceive. These

18. *Mon Oncle* (1958). Directed by Jaques Tati. France: Gaumont Film Company. Initial release 10 May 1958.

19. Philip K Dick, *Ubik* (New York: Doubleday, 1969).

20. Douglas Adams, *The Hitchhiker's Guide to the Galaxy* (London: Pan Books, 1979).

21. Gary Shteyngart, *Super Sad True Love Story* (London: Granta, 2010).

22. Dave Eggers, *The Circle* (London: Penguin Books, 2013).

technologies perpetuate a gendered form of power that regulates the productivity and reproductivity of women's bodies, ensuring that they are optimised at all times. The smart home isolates women, confining them, once more, to the kitchen as workshop. Surrounded by glass, as the new consumer-oriented material of the day, women's bodies are increasingly transparent, open to scrutiny and self-scrutiny in mirrors, windows, walls and screens. Here, we may find ourselves wanting and strive for perfection. Here, we encounter our reflection and our potential substitution by an ambiguous, intelligent, shape-shifter material that is striving even harder than we are.

Smarter homes

We need smarter homes in the political sense, and we need the politics of the smart home to catch up and keep up with the technology. Designers, engineers, programmers and developers should be trained out of their cultural agnosticism. Smart sexism, smart racism and all forms of social bias and discrimination are a shared responsibility and there is no purely technological innovation that will solve them. Design is a social practice and a form of social history, but that doesn't mean to say that it cannot be fun.

The future home of the 1950s generated its own culture of mildly satirical fun, including Richard Hamilton's artwork of 1956: *Just what is it that makes today's homes so different, so appealing?* Hamilton's collage literally crowds out the insular, interior space of the living room, opening it up to the objects and ideologies of the time, flushing them out and putting them on display. The housewife pulling a floor cleaner up the stairs is made newly visible opposite the voluptuous nude sitting on the back of the sofa. Hamilton's remake of this image, *Just what is it that makes today's homes so different?* (1994), replaced the nude with a female body builder, placing her opposite a bust of Margaret Thatcher – a new, more individualistic sign of the times.

Jacques Tati's comic film *Mon Oncle*, released in 1958, is both an endearing and an enduring satire of the functional order and efficiency of the modernist future home.[18] In its kitchen scene, a character from another era enters, pushing random buttons and making random sounds; he plays with a plastic jug, which bounces on the floor, and a glass beaker that (unsurprisingly) doesn't. Satirical science-fiction novels took over in the following two decades, with Philip K Dick's talking door that demands cash for opening and threatens to sue you if you don't pay[19] and Douglas Adams's obsequious elevator that lives to serve and derives satisfaction from a job done well.[20] The satire hardens in the era of smart tech, social-media giants and consumer capitalism on the brink of self-destruction: novels such as Gary Shteyngart's *Super Sad True Love Story*[21] and Dave Eggers' *The Circle*[22] flirt with the possibility of giving all this a final, fatal push. Comedy, satire and parody are, however, not necessarily at odds with ethnographies

23. Bell and Kaye.

24. William W Gaver, 'Curious Things for Curious People' (London: Royal College of Art, 1983), 5–7, citeseerx.ist.psu. edu/viewdoc/download? doi=10.1.1.458.1617&rep= rep1&type=pdf [Accessed 8 September 2018]

25. Oldenziel and Zachmann, 'Kitchens as Technology and Politics'.

of the home and kitchen that offer a cross-cultural analysis of real-life habitation and use in order to challenge the abstract ideals of technological innovation and ideologies of progress.[23]

Speculative design is one area of activity that spans these and other critical approaches to dominant, industry-driven visions of the future. William Gaver's 'The Superstitious Home' is one early example. Gaver reads the smart home as a distributed network of surveillance devices: 'Your toilet might provide feedback about your health, and your bed might track your sleep habits ... this information might be sent to family members, to carers, or even to retailers and insurance companies.'[24] He seeks to subvert surveillance and control functionality with a Heath Robinson-like device called The Home Health Horoscope. It uses 'shy sensing' to make guesses about the emotional and spiritual well-being of the home's inhabitants and to issue some relevant advice. Part parody, this design concept also offers ideas about how people might live with technology. Perhaps a horoscope reading that says you are isolated and aloof might prompt you to invite some friends round – and make some mess.

Interaction Research Studio, History Tablecloth, 2005

The future home has been appropriated by a variety of means and methods, and yet it appears to be back in the hands of a homogeneous group with a familiar, instrumental vision. The intervention of female user groups had some effect, at least until the 1960s,[25] but the smart home needs to be re-envisioned and redesigned from a feminist point of view. Let's get Janet and Jennifer out of here!

'Home' is both property and an emotional site. This fundamental paradox structures all aspects of home and is especially manifest in its kitchen. This essay argues that the home is a complex place that combines past and present, aspiration and nostalgia. Despite attempts to rationalise it and render it functional, there are aberrant and irrepressible elements that, like slips of the tongue, betray the individuality of those who dwell in it. Indeed, the word 'dwell' carries associations of lingering and delay – it is an activity never fully achieved. Creating a home requires attention to orchestrating unruly components, effacing signs of disparity – the joins, discontinuities and eccentricities that draw attention to failures of domestication.

Giorgio Ceretti, Piero
Derossi and Riccardo Rosso,
Pratone lounge chair, 1971

In the 1960s, the ludic potential of the home was explored by a number of architects and designers who rethought the domestic as a metaphorical landscape. The Pratone ('Big Meadow') lounge chair, a clump of giant polyurethane grass designed by Cerreti, Derossi and Rosso in 1971, imagined the domestic interior as a 'pastoral'. So, fifty years later, does Ronan and Erwan Bouroullec's Lake Sofa – and, although designed a half-century apart, both relate to the idea of the domestic interior as bucolic. By playing with scale and making furniture that derives from natural forms, the designers surrealise relaxation in ways that invoke playfulness and liberation into an imaginative dream – like 'the outdoors'.

1. www.thedrum.com/news/2013/03/22/aga-total-control-cooker-suggests-it-provides-warm-welcome-new-cogent-elliott [Accessed 31 August 2018]

The irregular, idiosyncratic qualities of home are threatened by modernising functionalism. The film *Mon Oncle* (1958), directed by Jacques Tati, was made at a time when France was undergoing a process of transformation from a rural economy to a modernised world of goods and services. The title is first seen chalked onto the stone wall of a typical Parisian street, where dogs and children scavenge and play to the accompaniment of street sounds and accordion music. We glimpse the geometric modernity of the starkly functionalist Villa Arpel, and see Monsieur Hulot greet a concierge and journey to his attic apartment by way of a comically random assemblage of passageways and stairs. The Villa Arpel, the home of his bourgeois sister and her family, is conspicuously lacking in irregularity, comfort and conviviality. Everything is said 'to communicate', but there is only spatial anxiety and malfunctioning devices.

The archetypal house is a lodging place for memories – where people grow and leave traces that sometimes linger beyond their lifetimes. It relates closely to the body and its boundaries. Gaston Bachelard's account of the conventional house describes it in terms of its 'verticality' – of attics and cellars – in which objects and memories are stored and deferred. Resistances to rational modernisation are evident in persistent 'returns' to period styles as aspirational scenarios, the fascination with 'traditional' materials and textures, and the pursuit of the 'homely'. In an advertisement for AGA cookers, a 'career' woman, her bag resting on an adjacent cabinet, leans against the 'traditional' range – the image is captioned: 'A Warm Welcome'.[1]

AGA Cooker
advertisement, 1970

The hearth

The kitchen, bathroom and bedroom are the most embodied spaces in the house. They are the sites of ingestion of food, expulsion of wastes and the exchange of bodily fluids – in each of them, boundaries are transgressed and negotiated. They are places where acts of physical sustenance and hygienic care are performed.

The kitchen is a portal to the future, the most technologically invested and the most frequently renovated space in the home. It is also connected to global supply chains and a space for experimental encounters with 'foreign' ingredients and cuisine. The kitchen mediates between the 'professional' and the social. It is a space for rituals, for starting the day, breaking fasts, necessary acts of restoration, the first conversations of the day, the piecing together of social integrities that are carried out into the world. It is also an emotional centre – the closest thing in the modern house to the hearth, fulfilling archetypal needs for warmth and what Bachelard calls 'councils of continuity'.

The kitchen is also an elemental place of fire and water, where food enters the home and the transitions from 'raw to cooked' take place. It is a place of wires, pipes, storage and

2. A term used to advertise early refrigerators. See Jonathan Rees, *Refrigerator* (London: Bloomsbury, 2015), 75.

3. Marshall McLuhan, *The Mechanical Bride: Folklore of Industrial Man* (New York: Vanguard Press, 1951), 98.

4. *Ariel: Poems by Sylvia Plath* (London: Faber and Faber, 1965), 14

disposal. The menace of decay and contamination are 'managed' by packaging and the refrigerated miracle of 'recreating Winter',[2] with its benefits of hygiene and abundance. The promise of the functional kitchen is to eliminate the 'naked lunch', to turn potential disgust at the 'raw' into the domestic events of the 'cooked'.

The 'kitchen of tomorrow' as a mid-century-modern fantasy was far removed from the dark, elemental spaces of past kitchens. Le Corbusier banished the kitchen to the top of the house to 'avoid the irritation of cooking smells', but commercial modernism conceived of it as the 'cockpit' of the home. The fantasy of the modern kitchen is concentrated in the construction of the modern 'housewife' as a 'mechanical bride',[3] morphing between users, devices and icons.

The pressure to conform to the irrational conventions of domestic efficiency is evident in the opening lines of Sylvia Plath's 1962 poem 'Lesbos':

> Viciousness in the kitchen,
> The potatoes hiss
> It is all Hollywood, windowless
> The fluorescent light wincing on and off like a
> terrible migraine
> Coy paper strips for doors
> Stage curtains, a window's frizz[4]

Resistance to the imposed role of 'housewife' is configured in the subversive response of feminist artists who reconceived the iconography of 'housework' in the *Nurturant Kitchen*. The sleek surfaces and gadget-filled kitchens of the popular imagination are

Womanhouse, *Nurturant Kitchen*, 1972

5. The *Nurturant Kitchen* was a mixed-media installation devised by Susan Frazier, Vicki Hodgetts and Robin Weltsch.

6. Temma Balducci, 'Revisiting *Womanhouse*: Welcome to the (Deconstructed) *Dollhouse*', ahis3320.files.wordpress.com/2009/10/womanhouse.pdf [Accessed 31 August 2018]

7. Museum of Modern Art (MoMA), New York, 1972.

8. 'Our architectures are the result of a desire to secure ourselves to the surface of the planet ... our anchors to the planet should be software, like songs or dreams, or myths. Abandon hardware ...,' David Greene, 'The Electronic Aborigine', cited by Simon Sadler, *Archigram: Architecture Without Architecture* (Cambridge, Mass.: MIT Press, 205), 178–9.

9. Coop Himmelb(l)au – architectural collective, founded in 1968 in Vienna.

10. Coop Himmelb(l)au, quoted in Anthony Vidler, *The Architectural Uncanny: Essays in the Modern Unhomely* (Cambridge, Mass.: MIT Press, 1992), 80.

reconceived as a hyper-feminised space, decorated with fleshy, pink cabinets and appliances, the ceilings and wall studded with eggs and breasts. It was the first feminist work to receive national attention when it was reviewed in *Time* magazine in 1972. The *Nurturant Kitchen*[5] was realised as 'a deconstruction of the myth of the white middle-class housewife as a satisfied, fulfilled domestic goddess'.[6] The pantry featured an apparently endless sequence of plates of food indicating the relentless, dehumanising, production-belt obligation of unacknowledged labour.

In 1972, an influential exhibition, *Italy: The New Domestic Landscape*,[7] displayed examples of contemporary Italian design, and also proposed environments that featured mobile kitchen 'cores' and explored the nomadic qualities of the new, dematerialised home, inspired by space travel and libertarian nomadic lifestyles. Far from the dark places of the primitive hearth, it proposed transcendent forms of minimalism or liberation from the mundane nature of domesticity. The future of architecture was seen as incompatible with domestic fixity.[8] Coop Himmelb(l)au[9] affirmed, 'Our architecture is not domesticated, it moves around in urban areas like a panther in the jungle'.[10] This invocation of danger and play relates to a long history of antagonism between the heroic impulses of modernity and the complex, haunted and symbolic realm of the home.

The un-homely

Sigmund Freud's notion of the 'uncanny' suggests that the most familiar spaces are also the ones most likely to arouse feelings of unease. The kitchen is a ritual space, in which materials become ingredients – 'natural' components that have been disinterred, dismembered and dissected are cooked in ways that render them social and temporal events, as 'meals'. It is a threshold that contains disruptive contamination and disorder. Packaging disguises the origins of most foodstuffs, but the process of eliminating 'waste' has now become a source of potential anxiety, requiring conscious and responsible ordering. Ironically, at the point at which new technologies, surfaces and devices have secured high levels of convenience and hygiene, there is more awareness and potential anxiety than ever regarding the source and destiny of the things that we ingest.

Surrealism, from its earliest manifestations in the years after the 1914–18 war, sought the irrational as a residue in everyday objects. The house, as a container for the most mundane of activities, was a recurring theme for the movement's artists and poets. André Breton considered functionalist architecture as 'solidified desire'. Tropes of play, repetition, juxtaposition and scale were manifest in the Surrealists' reconfiguring of the house as a place of mystery and unease.

The irrational potential of the everyday is evident in the mysterious, hybrid objects of Surrealism. Méret Oppenheim's *Object* of 1936, renamed by Breton *Breakfast in Fur*, makes strange the most mundane utensils. A conventional cup, saucer and spoon are coated with gazelle fur to create a dreamlike object that mediates the worlds of feminine domesticity, fetishism, sexuality, seduction and disgust. It is erotic in its concavity and texture, and its relation to the repurposed, phallic spoon. Oppenheim suggested that it corresponds to an image of femininity in the minds of men projected onto women. *Object* is disturbing because it introduces the realms of sexuality and the abject into the polite conventions of everyday life.

Frederick Kiesler carried out a similarly disruptive experiment with the structure and form of the home. He developed his 'intrauterine', 'womb-like' dwelling, elaborated over a lifetime of studies and models, by placing an emphasis on sensual and tactile perception. Endless House refuses to allocate spaces to specific uses, creating the experience of inhabiting an 'organism'. Kiesler explored ways of accommodating the cyclical rhythms of life, the 'meeting of all ends of living' – incorporating a range of sensations in a continuous 'endless' experience. The indeterminate spaces deployed varied textures and materials – sand, rivulets of water, grass, wood, heated tiles and changing colours – to promote and acknowledge different emotional states. The 'elasticity' of his forms was intended to generate psychological and emotional liberation as a strategy for disrupting the rigid, habit-forming cultures of rationalism and consumerism.

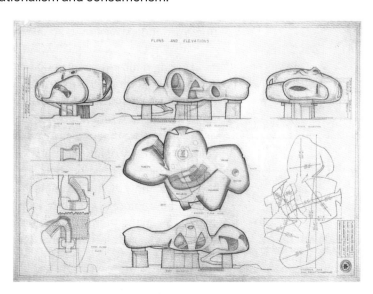

Friedrich Kiesler, Endless House drawings, 1959

The kitchen has always been a place both open to the outside world and profoundly intimate. Sharp knives, hard surfaces and household chemicals process unwanted matter. Body parts, dirt, impurity and decay are managed and eliminated. The anxiety-inducing nature of kitchens is exploited in a number of films of horror and haunting. In *The Shining* (1980), the vast kitchen and refrigerated-food store of the Overlook Hotel figure as a rational form of the

11. Pamela N Danzinger, 'Designing the Luxury Kitchen of Tomorrow Today', www.forbes.com/sites/pamdanziger/2018/01/12/designing-the-luxury-kitchen-of-tomorrow-today/#11a473d351c7 [Accessed 14 July 2018]

extravagantly anxious hoarding practices of survivalists and becomes a site of detention, terror and bloodshed. The well-equipped resort kitchen in *Jurassic Park* (1993) provides a hiding place where velociraptors prowl in search of food – a reversal of the normal order in which humans devour livestock. In *Poltergeist* (1982), an early, playful manifestation of the vengeful spirits takes place in the innocent kitchen, where dining chairs are animated as if at a seance.

In a number of video games and horror films, the eating spaces of the home are locations where humans themselves become food. In the film *Parents* (1989), the mid-century-modern American kitchen with its abundance of meat dishes is reimagined as a site of everyday cannibalism in the context of clandestine chemical warfare. A short film, *Kitchen Sink* (1989), explores the abject nature of plumbing and the anxiety-provoking character of the plughole, where the umbilical filaments of an unidentifiable, foetal creature are slowly drawn out by a lonely housewife. In the trailer for the popular video game *Fallout 4* (2015), an Alsatian dog wanders through a devastated kitchen/living room that intermittently fades into a flashback of an extravagantly equipped, futuristic kitchen. Other iterations of *Fallout* are amusingly aware of the alternative futures that prevailed in the Cold War years, featuring parody advertisements for fallout shelters and confident predictions about the preservation of the 'American Way of Life'. At the historic moment of the 'dream kitchen', its shadow equivalent was the makeshift, survivalist kitchen – windowless, underground, provisioned against an unknowable future.

Having it all – the synthetic future?
A time traveller from the mid-twentieth century would find the kitchen of 2020 surprisingly familiar, in spite of the continuing quest for 'smartness'. A recent Forbes article[11] described the ideal kitchen as 'a living room that you can cook in', with an emphasis on the domestic quality of fittings and storage spaces. Although there are many harbingers of safer, more intelligent and responsive kitchens, the increasingly digital equipment is contained by the 'timeless' design of 'traditional kitchens' invoking 'farmhouses', 'cabins' and variations on the theme of 'contemporary' and 'Scandinavian'. Wood, stone and slate feature conspicuously, and the popularity of AGA cookers and 'Shaker' cabinets indicates that a 'heritage' ethos frequently provides a comforting setting for the futuristic.

The ideal of technologically transformed living persists, however. The powerful fantasy of an omniscient computer deploying robotic devices to assess ingredients and process them into meals is still current. Food is conceived as processable through three-dimensional printing and devices that use cartridges for ingredients that can be superimposed and structured while being cooked, creating meals that can respond directly to dietary and biometric needs. In some scenarios, enhanced human connectivity is

12. theinvisiblekitchen.miele.com/2016/04/08/future-kitchen-design-technology [Accessed 31 August 2018]

provided by holograms. The Miele Invisible Kitchen, exhibited at Milan Design Week in 2016, was conceived by light artist and designer Christopher Bauder and his Berlin-based studio WHITEvoid as a nebulous 'virtual assistant' in the form of an intelligent, networked programme that guides, recommends and delivers complete meals. It is advertised as a place 'Where loved ones come together and where aspiring gastronomes come to experiment.'[12]

Miele, Invisible Kitchen, 2016

Irrational elements are present both in the desire to return to an archetypal homeliness and in the aspiration to inhabit a realm of magical devices. Both aspire to domestic spaces in which everyday tasks can be recast as intuitive and transformative. The kitchen is a place where the old and new come together, where customary and cybernetic pleasures cohere. The home of the future is likely to be 'smarter', more closely attuned to control and choice, but it will also seek affinities with the 'hearth' and the complex emotional and sensory pleasures of 'home'.

Emilio Ambasz

Afterword
Looking back to see ahead

In 1972, I curated an exhibition entitled *Italy: The New Domestic Landscape* at the Museum of Modern Art (MoMA) in New York. This collection of objects and interiors illustrated the remarkable design vitality that had recently emerged in Italy. Well received at the time, the exhibition was to leave a deep and pervasive imprint on the perception of design in the United States. For the first time, Americans were invited to regard design not only as a product of the creative intelligence but also as an exercise of the critical imagination. Visitors were to realise that design in general, and Italian design in particular, meant more than simply creating objects to satisfy functional and emotional needs: the processes and products of design could themselves be used to offer critical commentary on our society. At another level, the exhibition sent shock waves through the community of American designers. Here, they found themselves confronting another breed of creator, one unafraid of curves and taking unabashed delight in the sensual attributes of the materials and textures that he or she used.

For many North American and northern European designers, sternly trained in the Bauhausian tradition of deductive analysis, strict functionalism and rigorous pragmatism, the flair and panache of the Italian designers were little short of offensive. The fabric of their professional repression was so insidiously torn open by the creations of their Italian counterparts that they seemed ready to file a writ of complaint against Italian design itself for: (a) having created beautiful objects in complete disregard of all prevailing rules; (b) shamelessly seducing the public with these products; and (c) even worse, having seduced the offended designers themselves.

Today, we find that Italian design has spawned a number of gifted American, European and Asian offspring. Like their Italian colleagues, these designers have grown fonder of, and increasingly dexterous with, colours, curves, patterns and textures. No longer the unbending seekers of eternal truths after their Bauhausian ancestors, many designers worldwide have learned to make peace with the ephemeral.

However, it is another aspect of *Italy: The New Domestic Landscape* that resonates with today's living habits, and in particular with the subject of this book. Alongside the survey of Italian design that I presented in 1972 ran a series of new commissions – or 'Environments' – that offered speculative and often quite radical proposals about how we might live differently. Looking back, we might say that many of the issues they addressed still preoccupy us today – we might even say that some of their proposals were rather prescient.

Questions of compact living, nomadic living and the role of communication technologies were very much at the forefront of these designers' minds. Take, for instance, Joe Colombo's proposal for a Total Furnishing Unit, which condensed all the functions of the home into a single, adaptable object – it considered the problems of limited space in a way that today's micro-homebuilders are simply too conservative to entertain. Likewise, Ettore Sottsass's Micro-Environment, a series of connected modules that could be arranged completely freely in a space, imagined a world that was efficient, adaptable and released from personal tastes and habits.

Like many designers of the time, Sottsass anticipated a future in which 'one can put on one's own house every day as we don our clothes'. This notion of the life of free choice, unencumbered by domestic possessions, was encapsulated by Superstudio's collages, in which happy families roam free along a global grid that they called the *Supersurface*. Did these collages anticipate the internet and the networked living adopted by today's digital nomads, roaming from airport to airport and Airbnb to Airbnb? It would be easy enough to make that connection. Similarly, did Ugo La Pietra's proposal for The Domicile Cell: A Microstructure anticipate the trend of today's micro-apartments, in which the most essential features are our Wi-Fi-enabled communication devices? Again, hindsight makes that a relatively easy argument.

These were flights of imagination, provocations based on the designers' often critical view of society. But they were shown alongside the full spectrum of Italian production at the time – the real stuff of everyday life. Looking back on MoMA's 1972 show, we realise that it clearly marked a high point of Italian design as a freewheeling creative process. And many products of what we may, for lack of a better designation, call 'Integrated' and 'Alternative' Italian design have, since 1972, migrated from the museum to the marketplace. Once, these objects were fancied harbingers of upcoming social change; today, they have become fixtures of society. If they have not fulfilled the utopian promises of 1968, they have nevertheless enriched and improved the quality of our daily existence. If these objects have fallen short of offering path markers for our long voyage to a brighter, better tomorrow, they have happily performed a more modest role as pleasant companions in our daily travails.

These Italian products have given pleasure; performed faithfully; and, why not say it, they have tickled our fancy and flattered our pride. They have, in some small but true way, helped us through the day and soothingly seen us past the night. Handsome and wholesome, these products have served us well. If they have sometimes failed to move our hearts, they have always touched our minds and alerted our senses. What greater badge of honourable service can be bestowed upon an object and the culture that created it?

Biographies

Editors

Eszter Steierhoffer is senior curator at the Design Museum in London. Previously she worked as curator of Contemporary Architecture at the Canadian Centre for Architecture in Montreal. Her previous exhibitions include *Imagine Moscow* (2017); *Corner, Block, Neighbourhood, Cities* (2015); *Zoo-topia* (2012); and *Anatomy of a Street* (2010).

Justin McGuirk is a writer and curator based in London. He is chief curator at the Design Museum and has been the head of Design Curating and Writing at Design Academy Eindhoven, the design critic of the *Guardian* and the editor of *Icon* magazine. He is the author of *Radical Cities: Across Latin America in Search of a New Architecture* (2014), and editor of *Fear and Love: Reactions to a Complex World* (2016) and *California: Designing Freedom* (2017).

Contributors

Emilio Ambasz is an architect and industrial designer. He served as curator of design at the MoMA from 1970 to 1976, during which time he curated *Italy: The New Domestic Landscape*. During his long career he has received numerous awards and accolades, and there have been many exhibitions devoted to his work including those held at MoMA and the Chicago Art Institute.

Barry Curtis is a tutor at the Royal College of Art, and was previously professor of Visual Culture at Middlesex University and fellow of the London Consortium. He has written on architecture, film and design, contributing essays relating to exhibitions at the Tate, Tate Liverpool and the V&A. His current research is on conceptualisations of the future.

Dogma was founded by Pier Vittorio Aureli and Martino Tattara in 2002, and since the beginning of its activities has worked on several large-scale projects. In the last few years, the office has developed research that focuses on domestic space. Their minimum dwelling research team consists of Pier Vittorio Aureli, Martino Tattara, Marson Korbi, Barbara Mazza, Ezio Melchiorre, Marie Oudon, Lilian Pala, Antonio Paolillo and Laura Bruder.

Adam Greenfield is a London-based writer and urbanist. His most recent book is *Radical Technologies: The Design of Everyday Life* (2017).

Edwin Heathcote is the architecture and design critic of the *Financial Times*. He is also an architect and the author of about a dozen books including *The Meaning of Home* (2012). He is the founder and editor-in-chief of non-profit online design writing archive readingdesign.org and writes regularly for *GQ, Icon* and other publications.

Ben Highmore is professor of Cultural Studies at the University of Sussex. Recent books include *The Great Indoors: At Home in the Modern British House* (2015) and *The Art of Brutalism: Rescuing Hope from Catastrophe* *in 1950s Britain* (2017). He is currently writing a book about lifestyle tastes in 1970s Britain.

Dan Hill is an associate director at Arup, and head of Arup Digital Studio, a multidisciplinary service and strategic design team. A designer and urbanist, Dan has previously worked at Future Cities Catapult, Fabrica, SITRA and the BBC. He works as a visiting professor at UCL Bartlett School of Architecture in London.

Florian Idenburg is an architect and educator. He founded SO–IL in 2008 in New York together with Jing Liu. He is currently the Louis Sullivan Professor of Architecture at MIT.

Sam Jacob is principal of Sam Jacob Studio, a practice whose work spans urban design, architecture, design, art and curatorial projects. His recent projects include the V&A Gallery at Design Society, Shenzhen, *Fear and Love* at the Design Museum and MINI Living, a landmark project for London Design Festival 2017.

Sarah Kember is a writer, publisher and academic. She is professor of New Technologies of Communication at Goldsmiths, and director of Goldsmiths Press. Her research includes feminist studies of media, science and technology. Recent publications include *iMedia. The Gendering of Objects, Environments and Smart Materials* (2016).

Jing Liu is a founder of SO–IL, an internationally recognized architecture and design firm based in New York. SO–IL

creates urban spaces, buildings for culture, residences, and workplaces on a variety of scales and across geographic and cultural boundaries. Their practice is forward-looking: committed to making new architecture that will be adaptable to a dynamic future.

Thomas Lommée and Christiane Högner are a Brussels-based design duo with a clear political agenda. Their collaboration is one of the driving forces behind OpenStructures, an exploration of open modular construction. In addition to their activities as designers and researchers, Christiane teaches at the School of Arts in Ghent, while Thomas is a regular lecturer and jury member at numerous design institutions all over Europe.

Mary Miller is a London-based anthropologist whose research focuses on domestic material culture and everyday life in the home.

Barbara Penner is professor of Architectural Humanities at the Bartlett School of Architecture, UCL. She is author of *Bathroom* (2013) and *Newlyweds on Tour: Honeymooning in Nineteenth-Century America* (2009). She is co-editor of *Sexuality and Gender at Home* (2017) and *Gender Space Architecture* (2000).

Anna Puigjaner is associate professor of Professional Practice at Columbia GSAPP and co-founder of MAIO, an architectural office founded in Barcelona in 2012. Her ongoing research and writing on the 'Kitchenless City' has been

published in different forms, including in *The Quantified Home* (2014) and *Together! The New Architecture of the Collective* (2017).

Laura Ridpath is an MA student on the V&A/RCA History of Design postgraduate programme, where her interests include Cold War domestic design and consumer culture in North America and the Soviet Union.

Anya Smirnova is a curatorial assistant at the Design Museum in London. She holds an MA in the History of Art from the Courtauld Institute of Art.

Studio Makkink & Bey is a Dutch design collaboration, founded in 2002, that is led by designer-architect Rianne Makkink and designer Jurgen Bey. The studio's projects are diverse, including public space projects, interior design, product design, architecture, research-based projects, exhibition design and applied arts.

Deyan Sudjic is the director of the Design Museum in London. He was previously editor of *Domus* magazine, and founding editor of *Blueprint* magazine. His portfolio of publications includes *The Language of Cities* (2017), *Ettore Sottsass and the Poetry of Things* (2015) and *B is for Bauhaus* (2014), amongst others.

Acknowledgements

This book was published in conjunction with the exhibition *Home Futures: Living in Yesterday's Tomorrow*, created in collaboration with the IKEA Museum, held at the Design Museum, London, from 7 November 2018 to 24 March 2019.

Senior Curator
Dr Eszter Steierhoffer

Chief Curator
Justin McGuirk

Assistant Curator
Anya Smirnova

Curatorial Research Assistants
Giang An, Lara Chapman,
Uli Gamper and Laura Ridpath

Exhibitions Project Manager
Claire Corrin

Exhibitions Project Coordinator
Zoe Few

Exhibition Design
SO–IL

Exhibition Graphic Design
John Morgan studio

The Design Museum owes its gratitude to all the lenders of the exhibition. Special thanks to colleagues and friends who have generously shared their knowledge and advice to aid the curatorial development of the exhibition.

The Design Museum would also like to thank the following organisations and people:

Alan Cristea Gallery, Alessandro Mendini Studio, Anton & Irene, Archivio Ugo La Pietra, Pierre Avoine, Dimitri Bähler, B&B Italia, Beka & Lemoine, Bouroullec Studio, Cabinet Gallery, Aric Chen, Chris Beetles Gallery, Cité de l'Architecture et du Patrimoine/Musée des Monuments Français, Conran Foundation Collection, Michael Craig-Martin, CSAC Parma, Dogma, Drawing Matter, Dunne & Raby, EDGE Design Institute Ltd., Ignazia Favata/Studio Joe Colombo, Gian Piero Frassinelli, Yona Friedman, Friedman Benda Gallery, Alexey Ginzburg, Google, Jesse Howard, Industrial Facility, The Kaplický Centre, Professor Günter Zamp Kelp, Linder, Michele De Lucchi Archive, Mozilla Foundation, Marilia Pederbelli, Private Archive Hollein, Richard Hamilton Estate, RIGALI, Sadie Coles, Sheldrake Press, Natalia Shilova (Ginzburg Design), Smithson Family Archive, SPACE10, Stuart Shave/Modern Art, Studio Andrea Branzi, Studio Makkink & Bey, Luke Sturgeon, Superflux, Vitra, Zanotta Italy and Andrea Zittel.

The Design Museum is proud to partner with the IKEA Museum and greatly appreciates its support of the *Home Futures* exhibition.

Index

Note: page numbers in **bold** refer to information contained in captions.

Picture credits

Cover (clockwise starting from the top):
Per Tingleff
Ignazia Favata/Studio Joe Colombo
Studio Bouroullec
Courtesy of © Michele De Lucchi
Courtesy of B&B Italia
OpenStructures
© Gufram

Back cover (clockwise starting from the top):
© Vitra/Andreas Sütterlin
General Motors LLC
© Gufram
Jason Tozer
Per Tingleff
© Gufram
Ignazia Favata/Studio Joe Colombo.

Background via www.freeimages.co.uk

© Absalon Estate: p.152
© Absalon Estate/CNAP/ Yves Chenot: pp.150–1
© ADAGP, Paris and DACS, London 2018: pp.59, 63
© ADAGP, Paris and DACS, London 2018/Courtesy of CSAC, Università di Parma: pp.60–2, 64
Adrian Brown LRPS: p.57
The Advertising Archives: p.111
© 2018 AGA: p.286
Airbnb: p.262 (bottom)
Alie Design International Inc./ Microsoft: p.278
Amazon Inc.: p.263
© Andrea Zittel, courtesy of the artist and Sadie Coles HQ, London/Robert Glowacki: pp.146–7
Angela Moore: pp.156–7
Anton Gottlob: pp. 18–9, 44–5, 86–7, 128–9, 158–9, 196–7
Apex Tool Group LLC: p.171
© Archigram 1969: p.119
© Archigram 1968/ Dennis Crompton: p.271
Courtesy Archive Poltronova/ Dario Bartolini: p.201
Courtesy Archivio Ugo La Pietra, Milano: pp.31–7, 53, 83–5
Arthur Rothstein: p.141
Atelier Van Lieshout: pp.191–5
© 2018 August Home: p.121
© 2018 Austrian Frederick and Lillian Kiesler Private Foundation, Vienna: pp.202–6, 289
Courtesy of B&B Italia: p.212
Beetles Gallery, St James's London: p.100
The Beistle Company: p.207
Brigitte Hellgoth: p.39

Courtesy of BT Heritage & Archives: p.81
Courtesy the Artist and Cabinet, London: pp.126–7
Courtesy of the California Institute of the Arts Institute Archives: p.287
Canadian Centre for Architecture/ Unknown photographer: p.135
Courtesy of the Castle Howard Collection, reproduced by kind permission of the Howard family: p.153
Courtesy of the Charles Schridde estate: p.265
Collection Familistère de Guise/ Unknown photographer: p.248
Corning Incorporated: p.280
Courtesy of Cristiano Toraldo di Francia: pp.11, 69, 70–1, 78, 273
© Daily Mail/Solo Syndication: pp.13, 90–1
Courtesy of the Design Museum Collection: p.67
Courtesy of Dogma: pp.148–9
Drawing Matter Somerset, Copyright the Architect: pp.76–7
Drawing Matter Somerset, Copyright the Architect/ Craig Stevens: pp.72–5
Dunne & Raby: p.123
ECAL/Axel Crettenand: pp.98–9
EDGE Design Institute Ltd: p.139
Edi Eco/iStockphoto: p.101
Elena Bompani: p.80 (top and bottom)
Enzo Mari/Courtesy of CSAC, Università di Parma: pp.162–3
Eric&Marie: p.223
Courtesy of The Estate of Buckminster Fuller: p.266
ETH-Bibliothek Zürich/ Public Domain: p.247
Courtesy of Friedman Benda and Florian Idenburg (SO–IL)/ Daniel Kukla: pp.210–1
The Fuller Projection Map design is a trademark of the Buckminster Fuller Institute. © 1938, 1967 and 1992. All rights reserved, www.bfi.org: pp.48–9
Gary Chang: p.138
General Motors LLC: pp.113, 277
© Generali Foundation/ Mladek Georg: p.43
Gerald Zugmann: p.41
Gino Molin–Pradl/ Private Archive Hollein: p.54
Glasshouse Images/ Alamy Stock Photo: p.276
Google: p.219
gta Archives/ETH Zurich, CIAM: p.245
© Gufram: pp.118, 213–4, 230, 285
Haus-Rucker-Co, Laurids-Zamp-Pinter: p.56
Hiroyuki Hirai: p.258
Iftach Gazit: p.155
Ignazia Favata/Studio Joe Colombo: pp.133, 143–5
IKEA: p.225
© Illustrated London News Ltd/ Mary Evans Picture Library: pp.106–7

© Interaction Research Studio: p.283
iRobot: p.96
Iwan Baan: p.260
Jan Kaplický, Future Systems, courtesy of the Kaplicky Centre Foundation, Prague: pp.103–5
Jason Evans: p.24
Jason Tozer: p.55
Jesse Howard: pp.166–9
© Johan Fowelin: p.254
Johanna Pichlbauer: p.23
© John G. Zimmerman Archive: p.179
Jouko Lehtola, copyright exploitation rights with Artek: pp.164–5
Courtesy of Kartell: p.217
Ken Isaacs estate: pp.178, 180
Courtesy of Knoll Inc.: p.120
© Koji Taki: p.239
Luke Sturgeon: p.28
Margarete Schütte-Lihotzky/ University of Applied Arts Vienna, Collection and Archive: p.132
Masao Nishikawa: p.255
Courtesy Memphis Srl/ Lucien Schweitzer Galerie et Editions: p.215
Michael Beitz: p.227
Courtesy Michael Craig-Martin and Alan Cristea Gallery, London: p.124
Courtesy of © Michele De Lucchi: p.216
Mobile Life Research Centre/ Near Future Laboratory/ Boris Design Studio: pp.108–10
Moisei Ginzburg/Ginzburg Design with Fontanka: pp.134, 252
Morgane Le Gall: p.222
Naho Kubota: p.243
Nest Labs: p.125
Courtesy of Neufert-Stiftung, Germany: pp.136–7
New-York Historical Society: p.250
OpenStructures: pp.170, 173–7
Courtesy Orange County Archives: p.279
© Paul Tahon & Studio Bouroullec: pp.224, 232–3
Penguin Random House: p.10
Per Tingleff: p.38
Pinterest: p.262 (top)
Courtesy Richard Hamilton Estate and Alan Cristea Gallery, London/ © R. Hamilton. All Rights Reserved, DACS 2018: pp.114–15
Robert Lerner/ Whirlpool Corporation/ Library of Congress: pp.94, 275
Roger-Viollet/REX/ Shutterstock: p.269
© Ron Herron Archive. All Rights Reserved, DACS 2018: pp.50–2
Ronan Bouroullec: p.220
Courtesy of Russian State Archive of Art and Literature, Moscow: pp.26–7
Sheng Li Laisi: p.181
Courtesy of the Smithson family archive: pp.92–3, 140
© SO–IL: p.209

© SO–IL/Laurian Ghinitoiu: pp.237, 242
© 2018 Solemba: p.189
Sou Fujimoto Architects: p.259
Copyright the artist, courtesy of Stuart Shave/Modern Art, London: pp.116–7
Studio Bouroullec: p.221
Courtesy of Studio Andrea Branzi: pp.228–9
Courtesy of Studio Makkink & Bey: p.231
© Tiger Tateishi, Courtesy of YAMAMOTO GENDAI/ Courtesy of CSAC, Università di Parma: pp.42, 65
© Tiger Tateishi/Courtesy of CSAC, Università di Parma/ © Ettore Sottsass Studio. All Rights Reserved, DACS 2018: p.66
Todd Watts: p.240
Tomio Ohashi: p.241
Tommy de Lange: pp.22, 79
© Vitra: p.200
© Vitra/Andreas Sütterlin: p.25
Warner Bros. Entertainment Inc. All Rights Reserved: p.97
Warren K. Leffler: p.29
WeWork: p.272
Courtesy of Whirlpool Corporation: pp.9, 95
© WHITEvoid: p.291
Willi Baumeister Foundation, CC BY-NC-SA 3.0 Germany: p.7
Wurts Brothers/Museum of the City of New York/Getty Images: p.249
Courtesy of Yona Friedman: pp.183–8

Design Museum Publishing
Design Museum Enterprises Ltd
224–238 Kensington High Street
London W8 6AG
United Kingdom

designmuseum.org

First published in 2018
© 2018 Design Museum Publishing

ISBN 978 1 872005 42 3

Publishing Manager
Mark Cortes Favis

Assistant Editor
Tim Blann

Picture Researcher
Anabel Navarro Llorens

Editorial Research Assistant
Mary Miller

Editorial Assistant
Anya Smirnova

Copyeditor
Ian McDonald

Proofreader
Simon Coppock

Designers
John Morgan studio

Special thanks to John Morgan,
Adrien Vasquez and Florence Meunier
at John Morgan studio; Nicola Simioni
and Sara Negri at SiZ Industria Grafica;
Andrius Juknys and Mark Garland
at Thames & Hudson; and Elisa Nadel
and Elizabeth Gaffin at D.A.P. Many
colleagues at the Design Museum have
supported this book, and thanks go to
them all.

Distribution

Worldwide excluding USA and Canada
Thames & Hudson
181A High Holborn
London WC1V 7QX
United Kingdom
thamesandhudson.com

North America
ARTBOOK | D.A.P.
75 Broad Street, Suite 630
New York, NY 10004
United States of America
www.artbook.com

Printed and bound in Italy
by SiZ Industria Grafica